LABOR-MANAGEMENT RELATIONS

A Handbook
for Labor Relations Professionals

Charlene MacMillan

Labor-Management Relations: A Handbook
  for Labor Relations Professionals
ISBN: 978-0-578-90398-9

Copyright Sound Labor Solutions 2021
All Rights Reserved. No part of this book may be reproduced or modified in any form, including photocopying, recording, or by any information storage and retrieval system, without permission in writing from the publisher.

Logo concept and graphics: Annisia Cadogan
Cover art courtesy of pixabay.com

Chapter Quotations:
Loomis, W. C. & Herman, J., *Creighton Law Review*, Vol. 1, 1968 *Getting to Yes*, Fisher, R; William, U, 1991
Roberts' Dictionary of Industrial Relations, Roberts, H. S., 1994
Labor Agreement in Negotiation & Arbitration, Zack, Bloch, 1983
Black's Law Dictionary, 11th Ed., Garner, B. A.
A Handbook for Grievance Arbitration: Procedural & Ethical Issues, Zack, 1992

TABLE OF CONTENTS

Introduction — 7

**Chapter 1
Foundations of the Labor-Management Relationship** — 11

    1.1 The Purpose of Labor Relations — 12

    1.2 Rules Governing Labor Relations — 15

    1.3 Unfair Labor Practices — 22

**Chapter 2
Labor-Management Relations in Negotiations** — 24

    2.1 Why is Negotiation Necessary? — 25

    2.2 What Must Parties Negotiate About? — 27

    2.3 The Doctrine of Reserved Rights — 31

    2.4 When is Negotiation Necessary? — 33

    2.5 Decision and Impact Bargaining — 38

    2.6 Determining the Correct Approach to Bargaining — 40

    2.7 Bargaining Pitfalls — 45

    2.8 Good-Faith Bargaining — 51

    2.9 How Good Faith Affects the Labor-Management Relationship — 60

**Chapter 3
Labor-Management Relations in Practice** — 64

    3.1 Interaction of Laws, Policies & the CBA — 65

    3.2 Practice and Past practice — 70

    3.3 Collective Bargaining Best Practices — 75

Chapter 4
Labor-Management Relations in Employment — 85

4.1 Hiring — 86

4.2 Performance Management — 92

4.3 Dealing with Employee Issues — 103

4.4 Discipline and Discharge — 110

4.5 Just Cause — 117

4.6 Last-Chance Agreements — 126

Chapter 5
Labor-Management Relations in Operations — 128

5.1 Labor-Management Committees — 129

5.2 Job Classification — 133

5.3 Compensable Time — 147

5.4 Non-Compensable and Unpaid Time — 149

5.5 Working Hours — 152

5.6 Leaves — 157

5.7 Safety — 158

5.8 Work Rules, Policies and Changes — 160

Chapter 6
Labor-Management Relations in Conflict — 165

6.1 Approach to Resolving Conflicts — 166

6.2 Grievances — 167

6.3 Alternative Dispute Resolution Methods — 176

64 Dispute Resolution as Collective Bargaining — 179

Introduction

Most people understand that the labor movement grew out of a need for improved working conditions and to enable employees to have a meaningful say in the terms of their employment. What is not so readily understood is how this is manifested in the workplace. This book is intended to provide an understanding of the labor relations environment and how to operate effectively within it.

As a discipline, labor relations has typically been a legacy occupation. The management or union representative remained in their roles for many years, acquiring knowledge of the operations, the bargaining history and the best way to work with those "on the other side of the table". They became a source of information and insight for coworkers and subordinates, and often shared their knowledge with those who needed to continue the work after them. More recently, however, the field of labor relations has seen a much greater degree of turnover and churn than was historically the case. Today's union and management representatives are not only more likely to move around, taking different positions within or outside of their organizations, and even moving across the table, so that today's management representative might well be tomorrow's union representative, or vice versa.

This increased movement often creates challenges for employers and unions which must then assign or recruit individuals to fill those roles. In addition to relatively rapid and constant personnel changes, the field of labor relations is subject to legislative reversals, unpredictable influences, and the pressure of evolving public sentiment. Despite all this, the ideologies on which labor relations was built have endured, and they continue to guide the work even as practitioners come and go, as legislation changes, and as the public approves or disapproves of what it sees and hears.

This book aims to help those entrusted to play a role in labor relations develop the understanding needed to navigate this inherently complex environment. While much can and must be learned on the job, those who must play a part in labor relations benefit greatly by understanding the nature of the labor-management relationship, what makes it work, and what breaks it. Readers will gain an understanding the 'whats', 'whys', 'hows' and 'whens' that will enable them to be effective in performing these functions.

This book does not attempt to cover every possible situation a management or union representative might encounter. Rather, it addresses the most foundational and universal aspects of labor-management relations, with a view to equipping practitioners with the knowledge needed to effectively perform the labor relations function.

Throughout this work, the terms collective bargaining agreement and contract are used interchangeably to refer to the written, binding agreements upon which employers and unions based their interactions. When used on its own, the word labor refers to any organization or individual representing employees; the union. The terms management and employer are used for entities which hire and retain employees. Examples and illustrations are intentionally generalized and should not be viewed as exclusive, or representative of any industry, employer or union organization. Readers are encouraged to familiarize themselves with the labor laws applicable in the state, region and industry in which they operate to understand the parameters to within which they operate.

It is my hope that this book will bring depth of understanding, clarity of purpose and expanded knowledge to those who play a role in the labor management relationship, and that they in turn will educate others.

Chapter 1
Foundations of the Labor-Management Relationship

Mature, cooperative bargaining relationships require reliance on acceptance of the rights of each party by the other.
Loomis, W. C. & Herman, J., *Creighton Law Review*, Vol. 1, 1968

A competent practitioner has no difficulty navigating the procedural aspects of labor relations. In fact, in most situations, the necessary procedures will have already been established within the organization when he assumes the role, and the practitioner need only ensure faithful implementation in accordance with existing policies and guidelines. A truly effective practitioner, however, understands the reasons those standards exist and uses this understanding to guide decision-making.

The collective bargaining agreement, or CBA, is the predominant expression of the labor-management relationship. Antecedent to every CBA, however, are legal standards that apply even when there is no contract in force.

It is from these standards that the rules, requirements, and responsibilities of labor relations are derived. The goals, purposes and rules established by labor laws permeate every aspect of the labor-management relationship and should inform the manner in which practitioners approach their roles and engage in collective bargaining.

1.1   THE PURPOSE OF LABOR RELATIONS

The underlying purposes and goals of labor relations are not usually easy to discern. Many outsiders — and a fair number of insiders as well — view labor relations as simply the arena in which conflicts between management and labor unions play out, usually in contract negotiations, grievances, or strikes. It is true that conflict resolution is a key feature of labor relations, but it is only one component of the system.

The labor movement brought to light the need to protect employees and to ensure their fair treatment in the workplace. Labor relations thus emerged out of a need to balance the power and interests of employers and employees, and to mitigate the negative impacts of strife in the workplace, which can severely impede productivity, efficiency and economic resilience at the micro and macro levels.

In other words, labor relations provides an orderly system for managing the relationship between employees and employers, with a view to ensuring the continued viability of commerce and public service. The laws serve to eliminate factors which are known to cause strife in the workplace, and to mitigate impacts when problems arise. The overarching goals of labor relations are to protect the rights of employees, protect the rights of employers, and encourage collective bargaining.

1.11   Protect the Rights of Employees

It has been long recognized that enabling employees to engage in *concerted activity,* i.e., to act as a unit rather than individually, is effective in avoiding industrial strife. Employees engage in concerted activity for purposes of mutual aid, self-protection or negotiation.

The protections provided to employees engaging in concerted activity extend to their labor unions, as their representatives. While employees do retain some protections separate from their labor unions, within the context of the labor-management relationship, most of their protections apply to the labor organization as well.

1.12 Protect the Rights of Employers

Because workplace strife has the potential to disrupt the operations of an employer and may even impact the industry, its customers and the general public, the law aims to preserve the rights of employers to conduct business and engage in activities intended to meet their interests.

Collective bargaining facilitates effective concerted activity, but requires employers to give up some of their autonomous control of the operations. However, the benefits which accrue to management from having stability in the workplace and some guarantee of ongoing productivity are significant, and make collective bargaining a worthwhile effort, since employers also enjoy certain rights and protections under the law.

1.13 Encourage Collective Bargaining

Prior to the enactment of laws regulating the interactions of employers and employees/labor unions, the imbalance of power between the parties and the lack of restraint on employee activity often led to catastrophic results for both. Within the managed relationship, an appropriate balance of power may be maintained, and each party has the ability to act in their best interests.

Collective bargaining is the system used to meet these goals. It requires that parties recognize and respect each other's rights, and conscientiously work to meet their obligations within the labor-management relationship. The intended result is that employers and employees enjoy clarity as to what they may expect in the employment relationship and have access to corrective measures should those expectations not be met.

1.2   RULES GOVERNING LABOR RELATIONS

The standards and requirements governing labor relations are found in a variety of laws, rules and regulations established since the early 20th century. A proper understanding of the laws which apply to a particular industry or organization is critical to effective performance of labor relations.

The *National Labor Relations Act* (NLRA) of 1935, also known as the Wagner Act, exemplifies the goals, purposes and function of labor relations. The NLRA covers all employers except government, government-owned corporations, railways and airlines. Government agencies, as employers, are covered by the *Federal Service Labor-Management*

Relations Statute (FSLMRS) at the federal level, and by state and municipal regulations at the state and local levels. Railways and airlines are governed by the *Railway Labor Act* of 1926.

While these various regulations exist and function independently, and have different enforcement mechanisms, their overarching rules are fundamentally the same. Where the rules differ, they do so in recognition of the particular characteristics and needs of the environment they seek to regulate.

All labor laws define and enforce the rights and obligations of employees, employers and labor organizations.

1.21 Rights of Employees

In order to correct power imbalances, labor laws established the right of employees to participate in matters affecting their employment in meaningful ways:

- <u>Employees have the right to engage in concerted activity</u> for the purpose of mutual aid, protection or collective bargaining. Note that these rights exist within the context of employee groups. This means that any group of employees may act in concert to address needs, issues or conflicts that arise within the workplace. They need not be formally organized or belong to an established labor organization in order to exercise these rights. Employees have the right to form their own union, assist a union organization or join one if they so desire. An employer may not interfere with employees' efforts to organize and must recognize concerted activity as lawful and permissible.

- <u>Employees have a right to choose their own representative.</u> Once employees have determined they wish to be part of a union, they may choose the representative they believe would best represent their interests. An employer may not encourage, require or pressure employees to select a particular labor organization, and a labor organization may not retaliate against employees for considering or selecting a competing organization. Once duly elected, the union enjoys an exclusive representative position in the labor-management relationship; the employer must work with the appointed representative and may not bargain with other organizations on matters affecting that group.

- <u>Employees have a right to choose not to engage in concerted activity.</u> Just as employees may choose to be represented by a union, so too are they free to refrain from engaging in concerted activity. No employer or labor organization may force employees to become, or to continue being, represented by a union if they wish to end union membership.

1.22 Rules for Employers and Labor Organizations

The differing goals and interests of management and labor might create an illusion that they are held to different standards. But there is significant congruence in the rights and obligations imputed to both parties by law. In fact, the rules central to the effective conduct of labor relations are those which apply to both labor and management.

- <u>No Interference</u>

 Employers and unions are both prohibited from interfering with employees' right to engage in lawful concerted activity. No acts of coercion, intimidation or reprisal may be perpetrated by either party in response to such actions. With regard to organizing efforts, employers may not unreasonably monitor or police employees' organizing activity in the workplace; unions may not harass employees who do not wish to be part of a union; and neither may make threats or promises, intimidate or pressure employees into making certain decisions. To do so would be to unlawfully interfere with employees' freedom to organize, select a representative of their choosing, or to refrain from concerted activity altogether.

- Free to Express Opinion or Disseminate Facts
  Although labor and management are both barred from interfering with employees' organizing activities, both are allowed to share factual information with employees, and to give their opinions regarding organizing efforts, contract negotiations, or any other related issues, so long as those communications do not include elements of the prohibited conduct.

- Bargain in Good Faith
  Both the employer and the labor organization are obligated to negotiate in good faith. *Good faith bargaining* is an essential requirement of the labor-management relationship. Good faith is not easily definable but is demonstrated in all aspects and at all stages of the labor management relationship. It is revealed in the willingness of

both parties to acknowledge and respect the rights of the other; to engage in consistent and productive communication; to resolve conflicts; and to take steps to meet the essential goals of the labor-management relationship.

1.23 Individual Obligations

Rules that apply separately to management and labor concern their internal actions which affect employees, the parties' labor-management relationship or the stated goals of the law.

- Employers may not:
    o Engage in activity which has the effect of dominating or coopting a labor union, whether an established organization or a "grassroots" employee effort. Such activity includes actions which may appear positive and supportive on their face, such as providing financial support or other resources, but which have the effect of subjecting the labor organization to the employer's interests.
    o Engage in hiring practices that effectively favor or discourage union membership, or otherwise discriminate against employees based on union membership status. This does

not apply where the terms of a collective bargaining agreement require new employees to join a duly recognized union within a specified time period following employment.
- Terminate employees for exercising their collective bargaining rights.

- Labor unions may not:
    - Encourage or cause an employer to discriminate against any employee based on union membership status, except where the employee has failed to pay union dues and fees as required by the terms of a collective bargaining agreement.
    - Coerce a strike or other work stoppage for the purpose of forcing an employer or self-employed person to join a union or enter into an unlawful agreement. Unions also may not attempt to force any entity with which an employer does business to cease doing business with that employer in order to gain recognition for bargaining, unless they have already been certified as the representative of a bargaining unit.
    - Force an employer to assign work to bargaining unit employees which does not rightly belong to that unit.

- Charge employees excessive fees or dues.
- Encourage or cause an employer to pay fees or give other value for services not performed.

1.3 Unfair Labor Practices

Failure or refusal to meet these obligations, or violation of the rights of any party to the labor-management relationship, is a contravention of the law known as an *unfair labor practice,* or ULP. Such violations are subject to review by governing third party agencies which are empowered to impose sanctions and take corrective action against the party committing the unfair labor practice. These are to be avoided to the extent possible.

Rights	Union	Employer
Engage with employees for purpose of organizing and collective bargaining	✔	
Perform role as employee representative	✔	
Conduct business		✔
Manage the operations, determine methods and means of production, etc.		✔
Express opinions and disseminate facts	✔	✔
Receive information needed to engage in collective bargaining	✔	✔
Obligations		
Bargain with assigned representatives	✔	✔
Bargain in good faith	✔	✔
Provide information needed for effective bargaining	✔	✔
Execute and abide by written agreements	✔	✔
Work to resolve conflicts	✔	✔
Restrictions		
No unlawful obstruction of business	✔	
No excessive dues or fees	✔	
No union domination		✔
No discrimination based on union status		✔
No interference with employees' collective bargaining rights	✔	✔
No coercion, threats, promises or reprisals	✔	✔

Chapter 2
Labor-Management Relations in Negotiations

*People differ, and they use negotiation
to handle their differences.*

Fisher, R; William, U, *Getting to Yes*, 1991

If labor laws are the foundation of the collective bargaining structure, the agreements reached by the parties are its walls, at once defining the boundaries of, and protecting the relationship between, an employer and its represented employees. Negotiation is the process by which the walls are built, maintained, repaired and reinforced over the course of the labor-management relationship.

2.1 WHY IS NEGOTIATION NECESSARY?

Labor laws were enacted to correct power imbalances between employers and employees, and to allow employees to have a say in the conditions of their employment. The ultimate goal is to avoid or alleviate the negative impacts of industrial strife on the workplace, on employees, on businesses and on the general public.

Employees choose representation for a variety of reasons, based on what they believe to be in their best interests. The rights afforded by the various laws and regulations accrue to groups of employees who share a *community of interests*. Employees are deemed to share a community of interests if they perform the same or similar work, and/or share the same working conditions and claims to wages and other benefits. Other factors may be relevant in determining whether employees share a community of interests, including the impacts of major organizational or operational changes, bargaining history and even work location or supervision.

A group of employees who share a community of interests forms a *bargaining unit*. Agreements made between management and labor generally apply to discrete bargaining units, which allows for solutions that meet the particular needs and challenges of the employees in that group.

The determination of appropriate bargaining units and certification of representatives is often complex and may require the intervention of an oversight agency to define the bargaining unit. Once a bargaining unit has been formed, all employees who fall within that unit will be subject to the same conditions unless otherwise agreed by the employer and the union.

The labor-management relationship is formed upon *recognition* by the employer of a union as the exclusive, authorized representative of a group of employees. Recognition occurs as a result of an election process in which a majority of employees have signaled their desire to be represented by that organization. Alternatively, the employer may voluntarily recognize the organization if it believes there are justifiable grounds to do so, and that voluntary could benefit the parties.

Regardless of the reason employees elect to be represented by a union, or how recognition ultimately occurs, the formation of the labor-management relationship positions employees to engage in lawful concerted activity through their chosen representative.

The employees' representative is responsible for presenting the employees' needs and desires to management and engaging in discussions with management to secure their interests. Similarly, the employer's representative is responsible for presenting the employer's needs and desires to the labor organization and engaging with them to secure management's interests.

Collective bargaining is the mechanism by which these actions occur. Negotiation is a constant within collective bargaining and the labor-management relationship. It occurs with regularity and may take various forms depending on the circumstances and the goals of the parties. At times, negotiations are formal and regimented. At other times, it will be more informal and organic, occurring naturally in the course of business.

2.2 WHAT MUST PARTIES NEGOTIATE ABOUT?

Most labor relations laws require parties to reach agreement on certain issues affecting bargaining unit members' employment, and to execute a written agreement codifying those agreements. In some states, agreement is not required but parties are still expected to *meet and confer* on matters affecting represented employee groups. In either circumstance, the basic expectation is that parties actively engage with one another for purposes of addressing employees' needs and concerns, with a view to achieving mutually acceptable resolutions.

2.21 Mandatory Subjects of Bargaining

The issues parties must address in their negotiations are *wages, hours and working conditions*. These represent the matters most fundamental to employees' interests. These three categories — wages, hours and working conditions — are known as the *mandatory subjects of bargaining*. They are the issues on which parties are required by statute to engage in discussion and negotiation, and to reach agreement.

Although the mandatory subjects of bargaining are described using only three categories, the subject matter they comprise can be extensive. For example, the term wages refers not only to the rate of pay provided to employees, but includes other monetary elements such as bonuses, premium pay, healthcare benefits and uniform allowances. Hours includes work schedules, breaks, overtime provisions, shift changes, and more. Working conditions is the most expansive category. It can include anything from apprenticeship rules to certain workplace policies to cubicle size.

2.22 Permissive Subjects of Bargaining

Permissive subjects of bargaining are those over which parties may choose to negotiate but are not obligated to under law. They generally are workplace issues that do not directly affect employees' core employment interests. They include issues such as training, implementation of new technology and certain operational or organizational changes. Permissive subjects of bargaining provide opportunities for parties to demonstrate their commitment to collective bargaining and to making the relationship between management and labor as stable as possible.

Parties are not obligated to reach agreement on permissive issues and may not hamper the execution of a written agreement over matters which fall into this category. However, once agreed, any agreement reached on a permissive issue is as binding on the parties as those made on mandatory issues.

2.23 Illegal Subjects of Bargaining

The only matters over which parties are prohibited to negotiate are those that would violate existing legal parameters. These are known as *illegal* or *prohibited subjects of bargaining*. An example of an illegal subject of bargaining would be providing benefits to employees based on a protected characteristic in contravention of civil rights laws, or enforcement of union fees deemed excessive under the NLRA. Also included in this category are employment issues deemed by the state to be excluded from collective bargaining.

Practitioners should be aware that what is a legal subject of bargaining today may become an illegal subject at any point in time. As laws change, issues over which parties were previously free to negotiate may become barred by law. Such was the case following the Supreme Court's ruling in *Janus v American Federation of State, County, and Municipal Employees, Council 31 (16-1466; 851 F.3d 746 (7th Cir 2017)*, which overturned decades-old case law which previously allowed unions to collect fees from public sector employees who did not wish to be members of the union. With this change, parties in the public sector may no longer bargain requirements or procedures to facilitate such activities.

Appropriate classification of workplace issues determines the parties' obligations with regard to negotiations on those issues. However, whether an issue is a mandatory, permissive or illegal subject is not always as clear-cut as it might appear. While the categories are generally reliable, the specific issues they comprise may change depending on the state in which the labor-management relationship is established, the particular sector in which business is conducted, and, importantly, the manner in which they affect the employees or the employer.

For example, although *Janus* outlawed collection of union dues from public sector employees who declined membership, it did not change the legality of such activity in the private sector in states which already allowed it. And in many public sector environments, health and retirement benefits are unquestionably mandatory subjects of bargaining, but are illegal in others.

Most confusing, though, are those issues which tend to fall under the expansive 'working conditions' umbrella. As we shall soon see, whether a working condition is a mandatory or permissive subject of bargaining is often dependent on the extent to which it touches on core employee interests.

2.3   THE DOCTRINE OF RESERVED RIGHTS

One way in which the law protects the rights of employers is through *reserved rights*. The doctrine of reserved rights acknowledges that a business entity exists primarily to produce a good or service, meet the needs of customers and make a profit. It recognizes that those who own and manage the business have an inherent right to conduct business in a manner intended to meet those goals. Those rights may not be involuntarily abrogated. However, employers with employees who have opted to be represented by a union are required by law to engage in collective bargaining, and to reach agreement with the union on certain matters.

The agreements an employer is required to make effectively curtail management's inherent rights to unilaterally make decisions regarding its operations. Accords reached through negotiations indicate an employer's agreement to relinquish its unilateral powers in the matter negotiated and to the extent agreed by the parties. Any issues not agreed upon remain within the employer's prerogative.

These reserved rights are typically referred to as *management rights*, and will normally be identified within the collective bargaining agreement. While the specific rights vary from one contract to another, the employer is generally held to retain the right to determine what it will produce, where its headquarters will be located, and whether to hire or fire employees.

2.4 WHEN IS NEGOTIATION NECESSARY?

Negotiation is a consistent and ongoing feature of the labor-management relationship. It becomes essential when a group of employees is formally organized, and continues until the relationship is dissolved by the will of the employees, by a change in conditions affecting the ongoing labor-management relationship, or by a decision of the representative organization or both parties in concert.

Negotiation permeates all aspects of the labor-management relationship but is most readily observable when the parties are at the bargaining "table". In abstraction, parties in a labor-management relationship are always at the bargaining table; negotiation is the very essence of labor relations and the principal manner in which it is conducted. But there are times parties must, literally, come to the table to negotiate the terms of their engagement.

2.41 Initial Contract

The first expression of this occurs when the parties are negotiating an initial contract following the recognition of the union organization as the representatives of a group of employees. Parties are required to meet and confer, to reach agreement on mandatory subjects of bargaining, to reduce those agreements to writing and to properly execute the collective bargaining agreement.

Once the agreement has been ratified, no changes may be made to any terms without further negotiation. Some parties negotiate a *zipper clause* which affirms that the collective bargaining agreement is their complete and only accord, and that it may not be changed during the term of the contract. Some zipper clauses also incorporate practices not spelled out in the contract but upon which both parties rely and preserve these for the duration of the contract. The contract is considered to be *closed* until its expiration.

Zipper clauses, as well as agreement on when a contract is open or closed, are critical to the parties' ability to rely on the collective bargaining agreement as the definitive guide for conducting the relationship. Parties know what to expect and have assurance that their counterparts will not capriciously alter the terms of their engagement.

2.42 Contract Expiration

The labor-management relationship continues for as long as the union remains the recognized representative of the employee group and does not need to be renewed or reaffirmed as a matter of course. The collective bargaining agreement, however, is of limited duration, and is effective only for the maximum amount of time allowed by statute, or as agreed by the parties, whichever is shorter. Once expired, the terms of the agreement technically expire, but the labor-management relationship remains intact.

Because the relationship persists, some protections and benefits continue beyond the term of the contract. Practitioners must understand which provisions remain intact during the interval between the expiration of one contract and the execution of the next. This is a circumstance that can be fraught with difficulty and pitfalls for both sides, because it is not always clear which contract terms survive the contract and which do not. This uncertainty can be exacerbated by ambiguous or incomplete language in the expired which impedes the parties' ability to agree on how, or whether, it should apply.

As a rule of thumb, the following types of provisions should be assumed to remain in force after the expiration of the collective bargaining agreement:

- Any rights, benefits and rules based in statute. These include anti-discrimination and Title VII protections and most random drug-testing requirements.

- Any benefits specifically provided by agreement of the parties as accruing or due to employees beyond the term of the contract. One common example are wage increases required at specific intervals.
- Terms agreed by the parties which are intended to bridge any gaps between one contract or another.

2.43 Successor Agreement

When a collective bargaining agreement expires, it is deemed to be *open* and all of its terms and provisions are subject to change.

Prior to the expiration of a collective bargaining agreement, parties will usually return to the bargaining table to negotiate a *successor agreement* to cover the subsequent term. This time around, their discussions will be aimed not only at establishing the specific terms by which they will conduct the relationship, but on adjusting, adding to or removing such terms as their bargaining history and future expectations indicate may be necessary. Those changes, once incorporated and ratified by the parties, become part of the new contract which will govern the relationship for the life of the agreement.

2.44 Mid-Term Bargaining

During the contract period, parties will come to the bargaining table to address new and emerging issues, or ones on which it was deemed prudent to delay agreement. This is known as *mid-term bargaining*.

- Reopeners

    Sometimes mid-term bargaining becomes necessary because parties were not in a position to reach agreement on an issue during general negotiations for some reason. This may be because required information is unavailable (for example, when a wage study must be conducted in order to determine appropriate wage rates for new positions), because of anticipated or possible changes in the law affecting an issue, or to avoid unnecessary delays in implementation of the contract.

    In such situations, parties will often make a *reopener* agreement to facilitate bargaining over a known issue during the term of the agreement. These agreements override any zipper clauses for the matter to be negotiated, and clearly specify the issue to be addressed, the purpose or reason bargaining is required, and the conditions which would trigger the reopener.

- Workplace Changes

    Certain operational and organizational changes can also create a need for mid-term bargaining. Generally speaking, any changes that impact existing agreements between the parties, or relate to a mandatory subject of bargaining, will require negotiation, even if the contract is not open. This is especially true if the change is such that it would not be possible or prudent to wait for the next round of general bargaining. Some of the most common situations giving rise to mid-term bargaining include changes in policies, operational needs, laws affecting the workplace and organizational changes.

2.5 Decision and Impact Bargaining

The terms decision, or rights, bargaining and effects, or impact, bargaining refer to the approach the parties must take and the extent to which bargaining is required on an issue affecting the bargaining unit. The former is required for matters that affect employees' fundamental rights and the latter for those which fall within management's prerogative.

The management rights clause of the collective bargaining agreement can help parties determine which type of bargaining may be needed, since it identifies, broadly, the scope of issues which fall within the prerogative of the employer. However, some contracts do not contain a management rights clause and, even those that do, may not provide sufficient guidance in more complicated circumstances. It is imperative, then, that practitioners learn how to assess issues to determine the correct approach to take in bargaining.

2.51   Decision or Rights Bargaining

Decision bargaining is required where the subject matter at issue concerns a mandatory subject of bargaining. Recall that these are issues which relate to employees' fundamental interests in their employment and over which parties are required by law to negotiate and reach agreement.

Whenever mandatory subjects of bargaining are involved, parties must negotiate over the decisions that will be made. An example would be the establishment of a new employee schedules. Because decision bargaining is required, management would be required to delay implementation of the new schedules, and possibly determination as to what the schedule will be, until it has completed negotiations with the employees' representative.

2.52 Effects or Impact Bargaining

Effects bargaining, or *impact bargaining,* is appropriate in situations where management retains the right to make the decision, but must negotiate with the union over any impacts the decision may have on the employees in the bargaining unit. In these circumstances, management is free make its decisions and may move forward with implementation, but must negotiate with the union over impacts upon demand.

Impact bargaining is generally appropriate for permissive subjects of bargaining which do not necessarily affect employees' core employment interests. An example would be the selection and implementation of new technology. The employer is not obligated to negotiate with the union as to which technology to choose but may be asked to negotiate how employees will be trained in its use, or the process for implementation.

2.6 DETERMINING THE CORRECT APPROACH TO BARGAINING

In order to properly represent their constituents' interests, representatives must take the time to identify and understand their priorities, needs, constraints and any difficulties that have been encountered with the existing or prior contract language, if any. This requires time spent discussing relevant issues with those affected, gathering information, understanding the bargaining history, exploring alternatives, and repeating these actions as often as needed throughout negotiations. This represents a heavy responsibility and workload, but failing to take these steps will cause negotiations to be inefficient and unproductive. Beginning the process as far in advance of the start of negotiations goes a long way to ensuring the work that must be done can be completed as thoroughly and timely as possible.

The natural result of ambiguity in the classification of the various subjects of bargaining are questions of appropriate approach to bargaining. Some issues bear elements of both mandatory and permissive subjects and others, as we have previously discussed, either are difficult to classify or may be subject to change depending on the context. These are the factors which most often blur the lines between decision and effects bargaining though there may be others.

Questions regarding bargaining approach will arise in all labor-management relationships at some point in time. Because they go to the core purposes and functions of labor relations, these situations should not be taken lightly. It is important to remember that the manner in which parties approach bargaining on the issues is determinative of whether they are meeting their collective bargaining obligations. Failure to take appropriate action exposes the parties to unfair labor practice claims and creates conflict in the labor-management relationship.

Representatives should carefully consider the type and potential effects of the circumstances as they arise to determine the approach needed. Management representatives should avoid the error of unilaterally deciding a situation will not impact a bargaining unit and that communication with the union is therefore unnecessary.

Although some situations may appear unlikely to impact employees, there may be impacts which are simply not evident to management, but which may be brought to light once the union has had an opportunity to consider the situation from the perspective of the bargaining unit. When in doubt, it is best to provide notice and an opportunity to bargain before making any changes. In most cases, this will be a safe and reasonable thing to do.

2.61 The Balancing Test

When bargaining issues prove difficult to classify, it becomes necessary to identify some independent or objective standard to bring clarity to the issue. Within the realm of labor relations, the *balancing test* is used to analyze a set of circumstances and determine whether an issue is a mandatory or permissive subject of bargaining.

The balancing test looks at an issue in terms of its relative impact on the fundamental interests of management and employees. Issues most closely tied to employees' core employment interests or contractual rights are generally considered to be mandatory subjects of bargaining. Hence, issues affecting their wages, working hours and certain other conditions of employment will require bargaining on the decisions. Issues most affecting the employer's fundamental interests. These are largely issues which are centered on the nature and means of production, will generally be held to be permissive, and the parties may bargain any impacts to employees of the decisions made by management.

Note that the balancing test seeks to weigh the significance of the circumstances, on a relative basis, to management or the employees. For example, the selection of new technology that will radically change the way employees will perform their jobs will usually be a permissive subject of bargaining because it goes to the means and methods of production, a right normally reserved to management.

Although employees' working conditions will likely be affected in that the way they do their jobs will change, these impacts do not necessarily have a direct effect on their core interests if their wages or working hours remain unchanged. Because the greatest and most immediate effect will be to the means of production, the scale tips towards this being a matter for permissive bargaining.

The scale tips towards being a mandatory subject, however, if the issue is, for example, the establishment of a new work schedule intended to meet some operational need. Here, the greatest and most immediate impact will be on employees' working hours. This consideration will necessarily outweigh the employer's interest in establishing the new schedule because the schedule could not realized without affecting a mandatory subject of bargaining.

2.62 Third-Party Adjudication

Some issues are so complex that even applying the balancing test is ineffective at resolving disagreement as to the parties' bargaining obligations. In such situations, parties may seek a determination from a neutral third party by filing an appeal with an oversight agency. The balancing test very often will be the standard used by such an agency to assess the parties' claims, but it will be applied from a truly objective and neutral standpoint with a view to enforcing the applicable laws, encouraging the employer and union to meet their bargaining obligations and protecting the rights of the affected employees.

2.7 BARGAINING PITFALLS

In order to properly represent their constituents' interests, representatives must take the time to identify and understand their priorities, needs, constraints and any difficulties that have been encountered with the existing or prior contract language, if any. This requires time spent discussing relevant issues with those affected, gathering information, understanding the bargaining history, exploring alternatives, and repeating these actions as often as needed throughout negotiations. This represents a heavy responsibility and workload, but failing to take these steps will cause negotiations to be inefficient and unproductive. Beginning the process as far in advance of the start of negotiations goes a long way to ensuring the work that must be done can be completed as thoroughly and timely as possible.

At all points in the labor-management relationship, parties are required to negotiate with appointed representatives in good faith. While a failure to meet bargaining obligations may occur at any time, it is more likely to result from circumstances that require mid-term or ongoing collective bargaining. This is because, in such situations, the need for bargaining is not the result of a distinct event such as recognition of a new union or expiration of a contract; these are situations in which parties are generally vigilant regarding their bargaining obligations.

It is those conditions which derive from the ongoing bargaining relationship, operational activity and changes in the environment or context in which the parties operate that may present challenges. These situations may be acute or may emerge gradually over time until they reach a point where a need for negotiation is realized.

Representatives should pay attention to workplace conditions and changes, including feedback that might be provided by employees or supervisors regarding challenges or obstacles they are experiencing, and assess these situations in terms of their probable impact to employees, the employer and the terms of the collective bargaining agreement. This information will help practitioners identify situations in which bargaining may be required, and take the steps needed to ensure they engage with their counterparts to properly address the need and avoid the following pitfalls.

2.71   Failure to Bargain

For situations in which decision bargaining is required, an employer may be guilty of an unfair labor practice if it fails to negotiate the decision with the union. Failure or refusal to bargain effectively deprives the union of the opportunity to representative and bargain on behalf of its members.

Returning to our schedule change example, if management sets and implements the new schedule — a mandatory subject of bargaining — without negotiating with the employees' representative, or without providing the union sufficient notice and opportunity to bargain the impacts of change that might affect the bargaining unit, it may be guilty of an unfair labor practice. The same is true for permissive subjects of bargaining. Implementing new technology which is expected to drastically change the way in which represented employees perform their work without notifying the union in advance, or with such short notice as to make impact bargaining impossible or ineffective, may also be deemed a failure to bargain.

Unions, likewise, may be guilty of a failure to bargain if they fail to respond in a timely manner, or to respond at all, to the employer's notice of a change. This sometimes occurs when a union is strongly opposed to the proposed change or believes the bargaining unit will not accept the change under any circumstances.

A union's failure to negotiate with the employer, particularly on issues related to mandatory subjects of bargaining, will be an unfair labor practice. If a union believes a change or proposal is likely to be unpopular or difficult to implement, the good-faith response would be to explain the concerns to management and proceed with negotiations, even though they may be difficult.

A refusal to bargain also occurs if either party causes unreasonable delay or attempts to block or circumvent negotiations. A refusal to bargain by either party has the effect of increasing tensions by protracting unresolved conditions and needlessly disrupting operations. These outcomes are antithetical to the intent and goals of collective bargaining, and may ultimately harm both the employer and the employees.

2.72 Waiver of Right to Bargain

A union waives its right to bargain when it fails to take action after becoming aware of a set of circumstances for which bargaining — whether on decisions or effects — would be appropriate. This occurs most often as a result of unions failing to respond to requests to engage in decision bargaining or being slow to request bargaining on effects once informed of a decision or change.

There is no set rule for how much time must pass between notification and response before a waiver is implied, but there must be sufficient time for the union to determine the implications and provide a reasoned response. This might mean allowing some time for the union to gather additional information and talk to bargaining unit members before making a determination on how it should respond.

Often, parties will engage in some back-and-forth regarding an issue before the union is ready to make a decision as to whether to demand bargaining. Sometimes, where such fact finding requires significant time, union representatives will seek to preserve their rights to demand bargaining by providing a written response to the employer's notice indicating their intention to bargain as needed.

Unions may choose to waive their right to bargain over an issue when they determine there are no material impacts to the bargaining unit, where any anticipated impacts are not expected to be substantial, or where they are confident the interests of the bargaining unit may be preserved by other existing protections. Such waivers should be expressly communicated, preferably in writing, to the employer.

2.73 Failure to Represent

An additional pitfall exists for the union where failure to engage with the employer, or to demand bargaining in a timely manner, results in claims by employees that the union failed to represent, or to properly represent, their interests in a particular matter. Represented employees may bring such claims because unions have a lawful duty of fair representation. A *failure to represent* is an unfair labor practice. Such charges are brought by employees against their authorized representative when they believe the representative has not properly represented their interests or has failed to take action on their behalf in matter related to their terms of employment.

2.8 GOOD-FAITH BARGAINING

The essence of collective bargaining is its collaborative framework, in which both management and labor are asked to work together and to manage conflicts as they arise. Collective bargaining is unique in that it requires adherence not only to the letter of the law, but also its spirit, in order to be effective.

This cannot be accomplished where parties fail to understand or appreciate the intent of labor laws, or attempt to use them to take advantage of one another. In fact, the laws make such attempts illegal by requiring that parties act in good faith.

2.81 Elements of Good-Faith Bargaining

Good faith is not easy to define. It is largely context-dependent and is determined to be present or absent based on a combination of any number of factors that might apply to the parties and the situation in which they find themselves.

It is important to understand that good-faith bargaining does not happen only at the negotiation table; it is demonstrated in the manner in which the parties conduct themselves in the everyday course of the labor-management relationship.

- Willingness to Bargain with Designated Representatives
  Both parties are required to negotiate with the individuals identified as the representatives for the counterpart organization, regardless of their own opinions of those individuals. There are several ways in which this may be expressed:

  o *Recognizing and Respecting the Role of the Representative*
  Each party must understand that the other party has a legitimate role in the labor-management relationship, and with those roles come certain rights and obligations that must be upheld if the bargaining relationship is to be productive. It's important to recognize the role and respect the rights of the other party at all times.

  When a labor-management relationship is first formed, management sometimes struggles with the new dynamic, and it is not uncommon for management representatives to approach negotiations without an appreciation for the fact that the labor representative now has a right to be at the table. Similarly, labor representatives sometimes seek to assert their position in ways that show disregard for the rights of the employer. Attitudes such as these are a show of bad faith and will undermine the relationship if not quickly corrected.

Management must be willing to listen to union representatives and seek to understand concerns and criticisms raised. Labor representatives, likewise, must recognize that management representatives speak for the entity which employs its members and are there to represent its interests. The employer is entitled to have its positions, needs and concerns heard and respected, just as employees are. Mutual respect goes a long way to preserving the labor-management relationship and facilitating the achievement of the parties' various goals.

- *Avoiding End-Runs*

    A party performs an end-run when it goes over the head of, or around, the assigned bargaining representative to get what it wants in negotiation. It is an unfortunate truth that parties often overlook or discount the need to ensure their assigned representatives have the ability to perform their roles effectively. End-runs occur when parties believe they can get more from another individual, or simply because they or their constituents lack faith in, or affection, for the representative. While it may appear logical and advantageous in the moment, an end-run undermines the other party's position, breaks trust and ultimately impedes attainment of the very goals being pursued.

In formal negotiations, end-runs will often be precipitated by a party sending an individual to the table who lacks authority to enter into binding agreements on behalf of the organization they represent. This results in unproductive bargaining sessions and greatly stymies negotiations. Because parties are required to make agreements that will bind their respective organizations, and which will have far-reaching economic and other impacts, it is important to ensure that the individuals sent to the table have the knowledge and authority to enter into agreements on behalf of their organization. Sending a representative to the table who is unable, or unwilling, to reach agreement is a show of bad faith and increases the chance that the other party will attempt an end-run in order to get results.

- *Avoiding Direct Dealing:*

    Direct dealing occurs when an employer attempts, to one degree or another, to negotiate directly with employees without the union's knowledge or involvement. Direct dealing effectively removes the employees' representative from the equation and prevents the union from performing its lawful role. Direct dealing is serious matter; it is an unfair labor practice which can carry severe ramifications.

    In practice, many instances of direct dealing occur inadvertently, with members of management engaging with employees in ways which might appear benign, but which are inappropriate within the labor-management context. Avoidance of direct dealing requires a recognition of the role of the employee representative and the ability to identify issues on which management is required by law to negotiate only with the selected representatives.

Labor relations representatives play a critical role in preventing instances of direct dealing. Management practitioners can safeguard against direct dealing by educating managers and supervisors so they understand when and what types of discussions should not be had with employees, and by putting systems and processes in place to provide clear and reliable communication as needed.

Labor representatives must educate employees, help them understand the union's role as their representative, be responsive and establish trust with the membership so they feel comfortable going to the union for answers and information rather than seeking it from management when they ought not to do so.

- Meeting at Reasonable Times

  Parties are required by law to meet at reasonable times and with sufficient frequency to keep negotiations moving forward. A party that refuses to make time to meet for negotiations, insists on negotiation schedules it knows or should know to be inconvenient or inappropriate (e.g. insisting on meeting only after working hours) is effectively acting in bad faith. Similarly, a party that resists meeting at regular intervals, or schedules meetings so far apart that negotiations necessarily falter, is not acting in good faith.

- <u>Sharing Information</u>
 One of the mutual obligations of labor and management is to share such information with the other party as may be needed to fulfill their respective bargaining obligations. At the table, parties will require information in order to assess proposals they wish to make, or those made by the other party; to guide their responses and to make decisions regarding the negotiations as a whole. The type of information a party may need, and the situations in which they may need it, are varied and many, but any reasonable request must be honored by the other party.

 To ensure good faith, both parties should avoid inundating the other with numerous or extensive requests for information that place an undue burden on that party. While some reasonable requests for information are necessarily expansive, an attempt to overwhelm a party by requesting unnecessarily large amounts of information may be deemed a show of bad faith.

Requesting information unrelated to the matter to be dealt with, information that spans an unnecessarily extended period of time, information that is difficult to compile, or which the party already possesses may all be indicative of bad faith. This kind of activity has the effect of stymying negotiations, impeding settlement and frustrating the interactions of the parties.

On the other side of the equation, similar outcomes are earned when parties are overly resistant to requests for information. A party that is too quick to deny an information request as being over broad, burdensome or irrelevant will likely stoke resentment and hinder any progress in maters of interest to the parties.

Both management and labor are always free to ask questions and verify the need for information being requested. It is advisable for representatives to communicate with their counterparts when responding to a substantial information request. Through dialogue with the requesting party, representatives can better able to understand the specific information needed; explain any difficulties in sourcing or compiling the requested information; obtain reasonable concessions in scope and content; identify alternative approaches by which the other party might obtain what is most critical; agree to more reasonable timelines for fulfilling the request; and, ultimately, maintain their productive efforts in the matter with which they are dealing.

- Willingness to Reach Agreement
  Parties are not required to agree to any particular proposal made by the other party. However, both parties are required to consider and respond appropriately to proposals presented to them. Refusal to respond to proposals, turning down proposals without explanation or discussion, or refusing to move from one's position are all signs of bad faith negotiation. Parties have the right to hold firm on their positions and to protect and seek to advance their interests, but they must do so in a manner that does not hinder the process.

- Ratifying Agreements
  Failing to execute a written agreement may be a show of bad faith. If a party refuses, or is unable, to formalize agreements reached at the table, this severely undermines the labor-management relationship. The purpose of the signed agreement is to solidify those expectations by which both parties will abide during the contract

period. If agreements are not validated by both parties, there is no assurance within the relationship, and the parties are again at risk of the kind of industrial instability which collective bargaining is meant to avoid. Representatives should ensure they have the backing of those with final authority over the contract when approaching settlement in order to avoid making agreements that will not 'stick'.

- Ongoing Communication
In all aspects of the labor-management relationship, as in any relationship, communication is key. To parties who respect the rights and roles of their counterparts, and who understand the principles that drive the labor-management relationship, the need for ongoing and honest communication is clear. Also clear, are the ways in which solid communication supports the labor-management relationship and helps both parties achieve their goals.

2.9 HOW GOOD FAITH AFFECTS THE LABOR-MANAGEMENT RELATIONSHIP

The negotiation table is a microcosm of the parties' bargaining relationship; it is where the parties' willingness and ability to act in good faith may be readily observed. It is also where the effect of the parties' demonstrated good faith in the normal course of their relationship, or the lack of it, can have the greatest consequences.

Where parties have failed to act in good faith, the labor-management relationship is negatively affected. These negative effects then set the tone for negotiations, resulting in discussions which are excessively contentious, unproductive and end in impasse and/or strike action. Parties who have conducted the relationship in good faith tend to reap benefits at the negotiation table: disagreements are handled in a respectful manner, and the parties are able to resolve them; negotiations progress and they are generally able to arrive at mutually acceptable terms and achieve the goals of the negotiation.

The actions which demonstrate good faith during negotiations are the same actions that define it in the day-to-day labor-management relationship. Regardless of the circumstances, parties must always be willing to respect the rights of the other party and to negotiate with their assigned representatives without undermining them.

Timely and ongoing communication is key, and parties should always seek to find ways to meet their obligations to provide the information needed to allow the other party to perform its collective bargaining role effectively. They must demonstrate a willingness to resolve issues through negotiation and collaboration.

Whether or not a party will be found to have acted in good faith will depend on their ability to demonstrate these aptitudes over the course of their interactions with their counterparts. Any determination of good faith will require a weighing of those factors most critical to the issue at hand to identify whether the parties were making reasonable efforts to meet their obligations.

Representatives should always consider whether their decisions and actions are more likely to advance or hinder the labor-management relationship and choose those alternatives least likely to bring negative results. This simple act can help parties avoid committing an unfair labor practice, but concern for legal consequences should not be the primary catalyst for acting in good faith.

Acting in good faith pays dividends not only by reducing friction but also by making it easier to navigate conflicts. The need to establish and maintain a labor-management relationship that is productive and preserves the interests of the parties should be sufficient to spur representatives towards engaging with their counterparts in ways that help to establish trust, and support the ongoing relationship between the parties.

Chapter 3
Labor-Management Relations in Practice

Collective bargaining...includes the day-to-day activities and interaction between employers and unions involved in carrying out the terms of the agreement.
Roberts, H. S., *Roberts' Dictionary of Industrial Relations* (1994)

Effective labor relations practice is about balancing interests, understanding the context, and honoring obligations. The day-to-day work is where labor relations professionals have the opportunity to combine the 'science' of labor relations (labor laws) with the art that makes collective bargaining work so well.

It is important for practitioners to have a strong grasp of the nature, purpose and mechanics of labor relations and apply this understand in performing the role of management or union representative. It is not necessary to be able to quote every rule of labor relations on demand in order to do the work well, but practitioners should understand that some foundational rule, regulation or law will be implicated in every labor-management activity. In other words, practitioners must be aware that, for every situation they will be required to deal with, their ability to bring the rights and/or obligations of the law to bear will determine their ability the degree of their effectiveness.

3.1 INTERACTION OF LAWS, POLICIES AND THE CBA

Even though the collective bargaining agreement is central to the labor-management relationship, it does not exist in a vacuum. Effective practice of labor relations requires the ability to assess the impact of other laws, regulations, policies and established practices applicable within the working environment, and use this insight for decision making. Inability to recognize and apply relevant rules outside of the collective bargaining agreement could result in missteps that could have unpleasant consequences.

Suppose, for example, that a collective bargaining agreement contains a provision that employees caught sleeping on the job will be subject to dismissal. One day, staff members report they observed Employee X sleeping on the job. Under the terms of the collective bargaining agreement, termination would certainly be permissible.

Not immediately evident to those responding to the misconduct, however, is the fact that Employee X recently provided the employer with documentation of a medical condition which affects his ability to regulate his sleep patterns. The employee, though subject to the terms of the collective bargaining agreement, is also entitled to the rights and protections of the Americans with Disabilities Act (ADA), which makes dismissal solely on the basis of a medical condition illegal. Thus, despite the contract language, the employer would need to establish a compelling case that no reasonable accommodation could be made for the employee.

Now imagine that Employee X is a long-haul truck driver. State and local laws, safety regulations and other certification requirements will all come into play, further increasing the complexity of the situation. There are other complications which may arise in such circumstances, but this example demonstrates why it is unwise to act without considering all rules that might apply to a particular situation.

This hypothetical illustrates the type of complexity representatives are required to manage in the course of their work. It is often necessary to balance any number of laws, rules, regulations and policies that apply in a given situation and ensure the most appropriate approach is taken further, consideration must be given to the regulatory environment, the industry and the nature of the work being performed.

The foremost responsibility of the labor or management representative will be to uphold and enforce the contract between the parties, but this is most effectively accomplished when practitioners understand how the collective bargaining agreement is positioned in relation to all other applicable rules, and use that understanding to guide their response to issues. Generally speaking:

- An applicable statutory right or obligation must be met, whether or not it is addressed in the collective bargaining agreement.
- If the collective bargaining agreement defers to a policy, the policy controls. Parties have a reasonable expectation that it will be followed along with other provisions of the contract.
- If a non-statutory rule conflicts with the collective bargaining agreement, the collective bargaining agreement controls.
- If the collective bargaining agreement is silent on a matter, that is, it does not address the issue, the

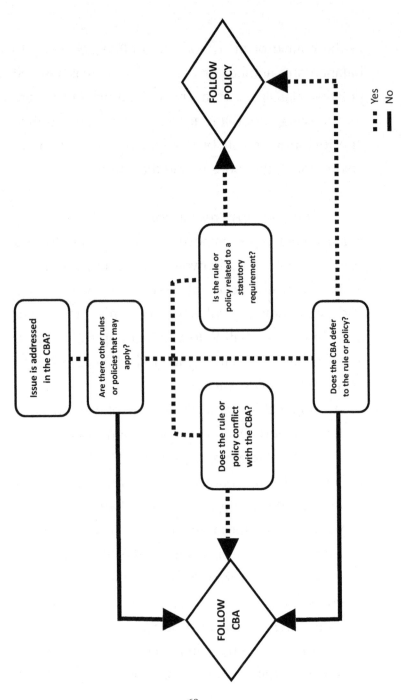

parties may follow any relevant rules or policies which exist.
- If the rule is law, and it conflicts with the collective bargaining agreement, the parties are obligated to follow the law and must cure the conflict via bargaining.

There may be other factors to consider. For example, if the employer is a local government or other municipality with its own ordinances, close attention should be given to which rules control. Some ordinances will defer to the terms of a collective bargaining agreement on issues affecting working conditions for covered employees, but will take precedence in matters on which the contract is silent.

3.11 Breaches

Clarity regarding which principle or principles control in a particular situation not only provides guidance in navigating a situation and approaching issues appropriately within the labor-management relationship, but also helps practitioners know what their options are in the event the other party fails to act in accordance with the controlling principle.

Where the collective bargaining agreement controls, parties may invoke the contractual grievance procedure to address conflicts. If there is an additional guiding principle that applies, such as federal law, parties will generally be free to appeal under the contract, under the law, or both. Where the collective bargaining agreement defers to a policy or law, that standard is effectively incorporated into the collective bargaining agreement, and parties may appeal violations of those standards using the grievance procedure.

Some policies and laws contain dispute resolution procedures which parties will often have the ability to adopt instead of, or in addition to, their agreed contractual procedures. Representatives should pay close attention to the specific rules or contract language governing appeals, as some will bar the use of certain avenues of appeal if other avenues have already been used.

3.2 PRACTICE AND PAST PRACTICE

In the world of labor relations, a *practice* is any action or set of actions in which the employer and labor union may engage in their interactions. It generally relates to the manner in with the parties conduct themselves in the labor-management relationship, but may also be used to indicate how they work with particular bargaining units.

A *past practice* is another matter entirely. The term "past practice", in the labor relations context, does not simply refer to something that occurred or was done in the past. It is not a literal descriptive; it is a term of art, and one that is not typically well-understood. Misinterpretation or misuse of this term, particularly by labor relations representatives, can bring undesirable consequences, so understanding and properly appropriating it is important.

3.21 Defining Past Practice

A past practice is defined by four main characteristics:

- The activity involves some sort of benefit for represented employees.

- The activity is deliberate and consistent. This means that the same action is taken each time a particular set of circumstances arises. Isolated, occasional or erroneous actions will not create a past practice.

- The activity has been repeated over an extended period of time. One-time or short-term actions will not be sufficient to establish a past practice. There is no precise amount of time required to establish a past practice. Whether sufficient time has elapsed to establish a past practice will largely depend on the context. For activities that occur with regularity, such as the issuing of employee pay cheques, a single year might be sufficient to establish a past practice. Where the activity is more occasional, such as providing employees with a Christmas ham, a longer period of time will generally be required.

- The activity must have been known to, and accepted by, both the union and the employer. Formal acceptance is not required, but can be imputed if it can be established that both parties were aware of the activity, and that they neither objected to nor sought to curtail the practice.

If these elements cannot be established, a past practice will not be deemed to exist. If a true past practice is established because it bears these characteristics, such a practice will be binding on the parties, so long as it does not contradict the express terms of their collective bargaining agreement.

3.22 Mixed Practices

If, given a particular set of circumstances, different actions have been taken over time, this indicates there is a "mixed practice", i.e., there has not been a consistent approach or response to those situations. A mixed practice does not rise to the level of past practice and is not binding on the parties.

3.23   Effects of a Past Practice on Collective Bargaining

It can be easy to lose sight of the implications of an established practice because the activity is often so entrenched that it's barely noticed until something needs to change. In fact, it has been said that the nature of a past practice is such that it is simply unnecessary to include it in the collective bargaining agreement, that "everybody knows this is the way we've always done it". Essentially, the parties come to rely on the practice, and it becomes part of the corpus of expectations undergirding the relationship.

The reason a past practice binds the parties is that it demonstrates the manner in which they have chosen to conduct a particular aspect of their relationship. The conduct of the parties, i.e., their bargaining history, carries a lot of weight in collective bargaining. Past practice is, effectively, an expression of agreement by conduct. This is why mutuality is so crucial to establishing a past practice; if one party was unaware of the practice or has objected to it, there can be no valid attribution of agreement.

A past practice cannot supplant clear contract language, but once established, it effectively alters the collective bargaining agreement between two parties. It can fill gaps in the contract language as the parties express what they consider to be acceptable with regard to matters on which the contract is silent.

A past practice may also help to clarify existing contract language that is unclear or ambiguous, since it demonstrates the parties' implied agreement that the application or interpretation of the language enacted through the practice is consistent with their original intent.

3.24 Changing or Ending a Past Practice

Once a past practice has been established, parties must continue to honor the practice until there is agreement to do otherwise. Either party may end a past practice by giving notice of their intent to do so and providing an opportunity to bargain over the change if necessary.

Parties will need to consider whether the contract in effect would allow such changes or whether they will be required to wait until its expiration. Contracts which contain zipper clauses will generally foreclose the cessation of an established past practice while the contract is in force. In such cases, the party wishing to make the change should notify the other party of its intent to end the practice once the contract has expired.

Sometimes a past practice needs to be changed or terminated because of circumstances beyond the control of the employer or the union. An example of such a situation might be where employees have long had access to free parking at a nearby lot. If the employer loses the use of the lot, it may not be able to continue providing this free benefit to its employees. Although the decision to end the practice may not be within the purview of either party, the parties may need to engage in bargaining to determine the best way forward.

3.3 COLLECTIVE BARGAINING BEST PRACTICES

As previously discussed, collective bargaining does not only happen at the table. Savvy practitioners understand that collective bargaining constitutes all of their interactions within the labor-management relationship, and that the manner in which they approach daily interactions affects the overall labor-management relationship. In addition, the way advocates manage the relationship will determine the level of confidence their stakeholders have in the collective bargaining process.

For employer representatives, their stakeholders include managers, supervisors, and others whose interests are mainly in the conduct of business. For union representatives, stakeholders are primarily union members — the employees of the entity with which the union has a collective bargaining relationship — and others who are part of the union organization.

3.31 Build Credibility

For the labor relations representative, the ability to be successful is closely tied to the ability to build credibility with stakeholders and counterparts on the other side of the table. Credibility does not materialize of its own accord, nor will it be imputed simply because of the position the individual holds. Establishing credibility takes deliberate effort and can be hard work, but it is ultimately one of the foremost determining factors of success for a labor relations professional.

While a solid understanding of the applicable rules, requirements and environment are critical to the role, being a good labor relations representative does not mean having all of the answers all of the time. It is important to be comfortable saying, "I don't know" if that is in fact the case. Over time, trust can be earned by being honest about the limitations of one's own understanding, and demonstrating a willingness to make whatever effort is necessary to learn, and to go the extra mile to obtain missing information.

It is important to always remember that stakeholders, for the most part, do not operate within the same frame of reference as the labor relations professional, and likely will not have the same depth of understanding of the mechanics of labor relations. For this reason, practitioners must take the time to educate their constituents to help them make sense of the circumstances and exercise good judgment.

The labor relations professional's posture towards others should be one of respect and fairness. It is best not to interact with employees, managers or opposing representatives in a manner that conveys disdain, a sense of superiority or unwarranted aggression.

As the representative's credibility increases, so too will their ability to develop and maintain productive labor-management relationships.

3.32 Keep the Focus on Employees

Employees are the common denominator in every labor-management relationship: they get to choose who speaks on their behalf and it is their expressed needs or desires which gave rise to collective bargaining within the organization. In the day-to-day grind of work, operational pressures and various conflicts, labor representatives can easily lose sight of their responsibilities to employees.

Management representatives often forget that union members are, first, employees of the organization. Union representatives sometimes allow their judgment to be clouded by other interests that may or may not be of benefit to their members. These are natural effects of the demands placed on labor relations professionals, but they should not be allowed to persist. Bringing the emphasis back to assuring the rights of employees will help stabilize and focus interactions between the parties.

3.33 Become Familiar with the Work

Representatives who are able to bring the most value to the collective bargaining process understand the working environment and the work bargaining unit employees do, how the work gets done and what the main challenges are.

Becoming familiar with the work and the working environment requires deliberate effort on the part of the labor relations professional. While some insight will be gained in the course of the work and in discussions with employees and management, this bestows a mostly arms-length knowledge. It is important to make time to learn about what employees encounter every day. In addition to increasing the representative's knowledge of the workplace, these efforts help to increase employees' confidence in their representatives and the role they play in matters that affect them.

3.34   Gather Information

In every situation, one of the most important things the labor relations professional can do is to make sure they have all the facts and allow them to guide responses to situations, rather than rely on conjecture. The process of gathering information will take different forms depending on the circumstances. Parties have a mutual obligation to share information that might be needed to fulfill their bargaining obligations, so representatives should view the gathering and sharing of information a routine and necessary aspect of the work.

3.35   Put Things in Perspective

Before taking a position on an issue, put things in perspective. Consider the rights of the employee(s), the rights of the employer and the obligations of both parties. Also be aware that the other party's actions might be influenced or driven by factors which are not easily discernible. The management representative might be under pressure to deliver a particular outcome, or the union representative might be attempting to balance competing demands within the bargaining unit.

Parties who have a good working relationship are able to share their constraints and concerns and use this information to navigate difficult situations in a manner befitting collective bargaining. However, more often than not, a representative is unaware of the particular constraints being faced by the other party, which tends to deepen conflict. Labor relations professionals must always consider the possibility that the other side might be under such pressures and determine whether a conversation could help to eliminate or alleviate roadblocks.

3.36 Take Time to Determine the Best Approach

There is no one-size-fits-all approach in labor relations. As a general rule of thumb, when dealing with situations in which there is clearly no violation of policy or contract, labor relations professionals should focus on problem-solving. When disputes occur, the focus should be on protecting the rights of the employee(s), respecting the rights of the other party, and preserving the relationship.

It will always be necessary to determine the nature of the issue, which approach is best and how to execute one's role. At times, the representative's role will simply be to provide support or guidance, such as in certain employee relations matters. Turning such situations into adversarial exercises harms both the employee(s) involved and the labor-management relationship as a whole. When conflict arises, or when involved negotiations, the labor relations representative takes on the role of advocate and, as is appropriate in such situations, works to advance the interests of those they represent.

3.37 Be Honest with Stakeholders

Employees will rely on what the labor relations representative says simply because of the role they play. As a representative for the employer or the union, there is an expectation and assumption that what that individual says is actually so, that the information they provide is reliable and that it is safe for them to act on their input.

Labor relations representatives must keep in mind that their job is not to rubber-stamp whatever actions their stakeholders wish to take. Rather, practitioners' responsibility is to help their constituents understand the reasons their actions may or may not be advisable, explain the rules, laws, contract language and other factors that must be considered, and be ready to recommend alternatives that might better meet their needs.

The practitioner's ability to effectively discharge this responsibility will be determined, to a large degree, by the amount credibility they have earned with their constituents. Representatives who have not established sufficient credibility with their constituents find that pushing back is a very uncomfortable thing to do indeed, and may seek to avoid it at any cost, but thoughtful and honest communication is critical to being effective in the role.

3.38 Be Consistent

Labor-management relationships thrive on sound reasoning and consistent application of rules. Representatives should resist attempts, or the temptation, to twist work rules or contract language to support actions not sanctioned by those rules. Attempts to misuse policy or contract language in this way breed confusion and mistrust, and undermine practitioners' ability to effectively resolve issues. Employees and other stakeholders need to know what they can expect from their representatives.

3.39 Communicate with Counterparts

The relationship between employer representatives and union representatives tends to be contentious by nature. Each is responsible for representing the needs and interests of a group of people whose views and positions are often at odds with those of their counterparts. Representatives can feel caught in the middle, and these realities can make the relationship between counterparts very difficult, but they needn't hamper productive interactions between the representatives.

One of the best and most effective approaches is simply to make consistent communication a routine part of executing one's responsibilities. The labor relations professional never errs by sharing information in a timely manner; asking questions to gain understanding of others' perspectives and taking them into consideration; communicating in a respectful and productive manner; and maintaining this attitude even in the midst of conflicts.

3.40 Don't Take Things Personally

The role of the labor relations representative is fraught with opportunities for offense. Representatives become easy targets for accusations, blame, insults and worse, simply because of the role they play. It is important not to take these personally, even when they are intended to be personal attacks. Such occurrences are best viewed in the context of the overall relationship, and the particular situation, rather than as a personal matter.

Labor relations professionals must be prepared to call out negative and counterproductive behavior when necessary, and do so respectfully and in a manner that does not embarrass others. Taking the time to clearly explain one's own position and reasoning, and keeping the interaction focused on the issue at hand can make a difference.

Chapter 4
Labor-Management Relations in Employment

Employer-Employee Relationship: The association between a person employed to perform services in the affairs of another, who in turn has the right to control the person's physical conduct in the course of that service; a legally recognized association that makes a difference in the participants' legal rights and duties of care.

Black's Law Dictionary, 11th Ed., Garner, B. A.

The right to hire, fire, manage employees, determine the size of the workforce and set standards of performance are widely recognized to be among the rights reserved to management, but parties routinely regulate many aspects of the employment relationship via collective bargaining. Labor relations representatives are often tasked with guiding others through issues related to hiring, disciplinary action, performance management and any number of other employee issues.

4.1 Hiring

Although management retains the right to make decisions regarding staffing and hiring, most collective bargaining agreements often contain language that affects several aspects of the employer's hiring practices.

4.11 Hiring Standards

Management generally retains the right to establish the qualifications, skills, experience and other requirements for employment. Whatever standards an employer uses to assess candidates' suitability for employment, its hiring practices must always conform to legal standards and may not be discriminatory. Parties will not be able, for example, to bargain language that would require or prohibit hiring on the basis of a protected characteristic.

4.12 Minimum Staffing Levels

Parties may agree to minimum staffing levels, with a view to ensuring operational needs and performance goals can be met, facilitating equitable distribution of work, and preventing employee overload. Where parties agree to such language, they will often also specify what corrections or remedies are permissible or required when minimum staffing levels are not met. These may include hiring additional staff, adjusting performance expectations or monetary penalties or compensation.

4.13 Job Posting

Agreements regarding posting of vacancies often include procedures intended to ensure bargaining unit employees are given the first right of consideration for open positions. Some agreements require that a position be posted internally, i.e., to a specific workgroup or department for a period of time before being more widely advertised.

Parties also may agree to the manner in which such internal postings must be made, requiring, for example, that openings be posted or announced at remote locations, shared with the union, or distributed via specific means. Some agreements go further still, requiring that bargaining unit candidates be interviewed, assessed and appropriately disqualified before external applicants are considered.

Within a closed shop environment, where only persons who are union members may only be hired into certain positions, those restrictions will apply even when a vacancy is opened to the public.

4.14 Bid Systems

Bid systems are another way in which bargaining unit employees may be given preferential treatment in the hiring process. Bid systems may apply for permanent vacancies or temporary appointments. This includes bidding for positions within an employee's same classification but at different locations or on different shifts.

Bidding allows eligible employees to indicate their interest in open positions and receive consideration or appointment by seniority. Procedures vary greatly in terms of the specific actions required, how employee eligibility is determined, and whether bid privileges are a guarantee of consideration only, or of actual appointment.

The ability to bid on open positions makes opportunities for advancement or transfer to other positions more accessible to current employees and can aid employee retention, improve morale and allow the employer to gain additional returns from its investment in employees' prior training and development.

4.15 Orientation and Onboarding

The orientation process is where employees generally receive their first instruction as what is required of them as employees. Many employers use a formalized onboarding process to acquaint new employees with their roles and the work environment, and to educate them on the organization's goals, methods of operation, policies and culture. Some employers keep onboarding fairly informal, entrusting the necessary activities to the employee's supervisor or manager.

Including the union in the onboarding or orientation process gives new employees a chance to meet their representatives, who can help them understand the role of the union. While a management representative may provide this information, allowing the union representative to lead this aspect of the orientation tends to be more effective. One reason for this is that management representatives are not generally in a position to explain the role of the union from the union's point of view, and this is a valuable perspective, particularly for employees who are new to being represented.

Including the union in the onboarding process requires deliberate effort and parties should discuss and agree on the parameters of the union's engagement with employees during this process, such as the timing, location and duration of this interaction, topics to be addressed, and whether both parties will be present. Some parties choose to allow the union time with new employees without the presence of management, while others take the opportunity to demonstrate their openness to working with one another by having both representatives in the room. Whether parties perform the orientation jointly or separately, it is important that it not be used by either party to criticize the other, or to engage in adversarial communication or conduct.

4.16 Probationary Periods

Most employers require newly hired employees to complete a probationary period before they acquire full employment status with the organization. The purpose of the probationary period is to give the employee time to acclimate to the work and demonstrate their ability to meet performance standards. It also allows management an opportunity to assess their performance, and to provide training, guidance and assistance in meeting expectations.

Probationary periods vary greatly in duration, but typically last between three and twelve months, and terms affecting represented employees must be negotiated.

Probationary employees do not have the same rights or claims to their positions as do employees who have successfully completed the probationary period. Collective bargaining agreements will generally identify which contractual benefits, protections and requirements do not apply to probationary employees.

Probationary employees may generally be discharged from employment for any non-discriminatory reason, or for no reason at all. Where an employee's probation is terminated for failure to meet expectations, the employer should be able to demonstrate that all reasonable efforts have been exhausted to assist the employee in meeting expectations, including clear communication of the expectations, additional training, constructive feedback, correction where appropriate, and reasonable time for improvement.

An employee who fails to meet performance standards during the probationary period despite such efforts, or who has demonstrated an unwillingness or inability to meet the organization's expectations, may be dismissed from employment. These employees will have no recourse to appeal since they had not attained standing in the position.

4.2 Performance Management

Performance management begins with the employee's earliest interactions with the organization. During the orientation process, the employer instructs new employee about the terms under which they will work, the responsibilities they are expected to meet, the benefits they may expect to receive, and the overall culture and values of the organization. Done correctly, the dissemination of this information sets the standards to which the employee will be held over the course of the employment relationship.

When organizational or job-related changes occur, when policies are added or changed, and when changes to the employee's role occur, expectations and standards of performance should be revised and communicated to again to ensure employees' understanding of the expectations is always current. One best practice is to review expectations at set periods, such as annually or semi-annually, but managers should be prepared to perform this activity at other times as well.

4.21 Setting Expectations

Expectations may be both organizational and job-specific. They should not be subjective. It is prudent for managers and supervisors to meet personally with new employees to fully explain expectations and give the employee an opportunity to ask questions and gain clarity on what will be required of them. This is critical to proper performance management; this interaction between employee and supervisor sets the tone for their working relationship and helps to establish mutual understanding of what they can expect from one another.

While the setting of expectations and determination of performance standards remains a management prerogative, parties may choose to bargain, to one degree or another, over aspects of these standards.

Organizational expectations include the rules, policies and requirements that have been set for all employees, regardless of rank or role. They include rules related to matters such as anti-harassment, time reporting, and safety.

Employees are also entitled to clarity regarding their roles, the job-specific expectations to which they will be held, and the standards by which their performance will be measured. Managers and supervisors must clearly define:
- The employee's position and its purpose in the organization.

- Day-to-day and periodic tasks that must be completed and timelines for completion.
- Guidelines for carrying out tasks, and aspects of the work in which the employee will have discretion.
- Specific deliverables, production or service goals, and/or expected outcomes.
- How they are to handle challenges to meeting those standards.
- Reporting relationships and what communication is expected.
- Any rules for performance or conduct that apply within the workgroup or that might be related to their specific responsibilities.

4.22 Training

Training is a means of establishing and communicating expectations while also equipping employees to meet those expectations. Employers are obligated to provide an appropriate level of training to all employees to assist them in meeting the standards set for their position, and as employees of the organization.

Generally speaking, training will be selected, or approved, and provided by management as a unilateral action, but it is not uncommon for parties to agree to certain conditions regarding training for bargaining unit members. Some parties establish apprenticeship or other developmental training programs as a joint effort, which become a significant aspect of union members' employment and advancement in the organization.

4.23 Performance Management Systems

Setting clear, objective expectations and communicating those expectations are critical components of effective performance management. Also required are timely feedback to employees about their performance related to established standards, suitable rewards for meeting or exceeding expectations, and effective means for addressing and correcting unsatisfactory performance.

Performance management systems focused solely on management and assessment of performance, without any impact to wages or employment status, are often implemented unilaterally by the employer, although unions are free to request bargaining on any impacts they may identify.

These types of systems aim only to ensure established production or performance standards are met. Alternatively, the performance management system may also be used to determine important employment elements, such as pay changes, bonuses, or even whether an individual will retain their position. Because this approach directly affects employees' wages and working conditions, this type of system will require negotiation between the parties.

4.24 Performance Reviews

Employees' performance must be assessed against the expectations that have been established and properly communicated to them. They should not be based on expectations of which the employee has not previously been made aware.

Leaders should not wait until the review meeting to let employees know how they are doing. Proper supervision requires ongoing feedback and adjustment to ensure the employee has all the information and resources they need in order to meet expectations. Absent this ongoing feedback, an employee may be unaware of ways in which they are failing to meet workplace expectations and miss opportunities to correct their performance. Similarly, employees may not know what things they are doing particularly well and may therefore miss opportunities to incorporate those actions or approaches and further improve their performance. Supervisors may choose the manner and timing for providing this ongoing feedback, but must ensure employees receive no surprises during the performance review process.

The formal review meeting is an opportunity for supervisors and employees to have a productive discussion about what is going well and what is not, and to plan for the upcoming evaluation period. If expectations or priorities must change, the employee should leave the meeting with a clear understanding of what is expected from that point forward. The performance review period is also an excellent juncture at which to identify developmental opportunities for the employee, and to plan for additional training to support their development.

Sometimes, such as where the relationship between the employee and the supervisor is difficult, where the employee is experiencing other challenges, or when there have been significant changes in the work or the working environment, an employee may request a union representative to be present at the performance review meeting. Parties should seek to accommodate those requests wherever possible, so long as it is not precluded by the collective bargaining agreement.

4.25 Addressing Poor Performance

When an employee is not meeting workplace expectations, the employer's first response should be to ensure proper performance management is taking place, and provide such additional support and training as might be needed. Where these have been shown to be ineffective at improving an employee's performance, other actions must be taken.

- Reset Expectations

   The first step in addressing a performance deficiency should be communication. Expectations may be reset at any time, either to address specific concerns or simply as a reminder to employees of what is expected of them. Supervisors should clearly articulate the specific expectations not being met, describe what has been observed, explain why it fails to meet expected standards and reiterate what is considered acceptable.

   In many cases, a brief reminder delivered by email or other written form is sufficient to reset expectations. However, discussing the concerns with the employee creates opportunities to understand their perspective on what has been observed and any reasons therefor. Dialogue between supervisor and employee should occur as soon as it becomes clear that regular, ongoing feedback has been ineffective at bringing change. Armed with this information, the supervisor may be able to help resolve concerns by removing obstacles or remediating challenges the employee has been experiencing. In other cases, the employee will be the one with the power to change their behavior or performance, and the supervisor must ensure they understand that they will be held accountable for doing so.

Timeliness is an important fact when managing performance or behavioral concerns. The sooner they are communicated to the employee, the more likely this effort will be effective at curbing unsatisfactory conduct. Such conduct, observed by managers or supervisors but not addressed, will likely come to be seen as accepted or condoned by management, and will be all the more difficult to correct later on.

- Provide Additional Training

Training is a meaningful way to address performance deficiencies which are the result of inadequate skills or understanding. Supervisors, employees, and unions may all be in a position to identify training needs and suggest options to help improve performance.

Training may take the form of a formalized program, or may involve mentoring, coaching, or other on-the-job training by the supervisor or a fellow employee. Whatever form of remedial training is used, it should be tailored to address the specific skill or performance gaps that have been observed, and employees should be allowed sufficient time to demonstrate improvement following completion of the training.

- Implement a Remedial Plan
When all reasonable measures have been taken, and the employee has been provided with all resources needed to meet standards but still fails to do so, they may be placed on a remedial plan, often called a corrective action plan or performance improvement plan. A well-developed remedial plan is a tool that enables employees and supervisors to take practical steps to correct deficiencies.

A remedial plan generally includes several components. First, it takes the resetting of expectations further by breaking down tasks, activities and responsibilities into discrete components, and articulating specific deliverables, timelines, outcomes, or goals that must be met, usually within a specified time period. It may also require periodic review meetings with the supervisor or other forms of reporting, performance monitoring or checkoffs. Demonstration of continued acceptable performance will be required before the deficiency will be deemed to have been corrected. Finally, a remedial plan should be clear regarding potential consequences should the requirements of the plan not be met.

4.26 Uncorrected Performance Deficiencies

Where all efforts to address poor performance have failed to bring about a sufficient improvement, management will look to other measures to resolve the situation. For newly hired employees, this will likely result in a probationary separation from employment. For regular employees, disciplinary action may be taken. However, there are circumstances in which disciplinary action or removal may not be the most appropriate response to uncorrected performance. In such situations, parties may consider other non-disciplinary resolutions.

- Reassignment: Effective performance management has the ability to reveal mismatches in employees' skills and abilities and the requirements of a position. No amount of training or corrective action may be effective at helping the employee meet expectations if they simply lack the aptitudes necessary to do so. In some such cases, the employer may consider moving the employee to a position more suited to their abilities, and in which they might have a better chance at being successful.

Represented employees in such situations may benefit from contract language which specifies how aspects of their employment will be affected, such as seniority, bid eligibility, and so on.

- Voluntary Reassignment
  In some cases, an employee may recognize their unsuitability for the position and may request reassignment or transfer on a voluntary basis. Where this is done, the employer should ensure the reassignment is documented as a non-disciplinary action, so that it will not later be held against the employee. Voluntary reassignments or transfers will generally be provided for in the collective bargaining, or in the employer's policies.

4.3 DEALING WITH EMPLOYEE ISSUES

Employees often experience personal circumstances of which the employer may be unaware until they begin to influence an employees conduct and performance in the workplace. The number and types of employee issues that may show up in any workplace are too many and too varied to cover comprehensively in this book, but they run the gamut from health issues to relationship issues to legal trouble and everything in between. The employer and the union generally have no role in or control over employees' personal circumstances and are not entitled to know what they are.

Because employees have a right to privacy, and because inappropriate intrusion into employees' personal matters could expose them to liability, parties should avoid getting involved in personal matters unnecessarily. However, when personal issues spill over into the workplace, the employer and union may be obligated to act.

The right of employers and unions to be involved in employees' personal issues is limited to addressing actual impacts to the employee's conduct or performance in the workplace, such as absenteeism, tardiness, difficult interactions with coworkers, and declining performance. Proper response involves gathering the facts, properly assessing the situation, understanding which rules, laws and policies apply, and determining the most appropriate and effective approach to responding to the impacts that can be observed in the workplace.

Issues arising from personal individual circumstances must be handled with care and sensitivity. They should be approached with the highest degree of confidentiality, and representatives should avoid sharing information with coworkers and others in the workplace who have no role in managing them. Although the onus for managing employee issues will fall largely on the employer, union representatives play a role in helping employees understand their rights and responsibilities, and may provide support throughout the process.

4.31 Common Employee Issues

The most common employee issues with which labor relations representatives must deal include disability, family and medical issues, substance abuse, mental health issues, and legal troubles, some of which may occur concurrently.

Practitioners should recognize that employees dealing with these types of issues are often anxious, worried and confused about what they can and cannot do, and may need direction and support.

- <u>Disability and Reasonable Accommodation:</u>
  Whether employees come to the workplace with disabilities and varying accommodation needs or develop them during the course of their employment, the employer is obligated by law to make reasonable accommodations which will allow them to perform the critical functions of their positions.

  While most employees will engage in the interactive accommodations process without involving the union, some employees may request that their representative be involved. In such cases, the employer should ask the employee to certify whether and to what extent they would like the union representative to have access to their medical information in order to protect their privacy. The union and the employee should agree between them whether the union representative is participating as an advocate and spokesperson for the employee, or whether they will take a more hands-off approach and provide assistance only when needed.

Because accommodations are highly situation-specific, both parties should avoid making representations or guarantees prior to obtaining all necessary information. Union representatives should avoid making the mistake of assuring employees they are entitled to a specific accommodation, and employer representatives should be prepared to explain the employer's reasoning for any decisions made.

There generally is no one "right" way to accommodate an employee's disability needs, and the best solution is more likely to unfold over time rather than be immediately obvious. For these reasons, it is important to remember that, even though the employer and the employee or the union may disagree as to the approach being taken, this in itself is not tantamount to a violation of the employee's rights. The law allows wide latitude for determining appropriate accommodations.

While the process is ongoing, parties should avoid approaching these situations with an adversarial mindset. To do so is to set the stage for unnecessary conflict that can prolong the process, delay resolution, confuse the employee and negatively impact the employee.

- Family & Medical Issues

    The law recognizes that employees may sometimes need time away from work to care for family members or take care of their own medical, parental or domestic violence related needs. This is another area in which legal requirements must be met and for which employers generally have well-developed systems. Employees will be required to meet leave requirements, to adhere to the leave as approved, and refrain from abusing it.

    Practitioners should be prepared to respond to questions and provide accurate information and guidance regarding these requirements and how the leaves work. Because leaves, and their administration, can sometimes be complex, so representatives should enlist the help of staff members whose role is to manage these types of issues to ensure they provide accurate information and helpful guidance.

- Substance Abuse

    Employers become aware of substance abuse issues, usually, in one of two ways: 1) the employee is involved in an incident in the workplace or exhibits behavior that leads a substance use evaluation; or 2) the employee self-discloses the abuse with a view to obtaining assistance or avoiding disciplinary action.

Substance abuse creates concerns for the safety of the employee and others in the workplace, particularly if they are employed in a safety-sensitive role, and may affect the employee's qualification or fitness to continue in the position. Where an employee's substance abuse has been discovered due to some incident in the workplace, the most common response is disciplinary action. Where the employee has disclosed the abuse of their own volition, both parties should work to provide support to help the employee deal with the problem so that they may return to effective functioning as quickly as possible.

- Mental Health Issues
  This can be a thorny area to deal with because it is not always clear that an employee may be suffering with a mental health issue. Often, by the time such issues garner enough attention to

require action by the employer or the union, the employee is likely facing disciplinary action.

Where such a condition is confirmed, the employer may need to embark on an interactive process to identify appropriate accommodations or, if accommodation is not possible, to find alternative resolutions.

Depending on the circumstances, the employer may request or require the employee to undergo a mental health fitness for duty assessment to determine whether they are experiencing a condition that legitimately affects their functioning in the workplace, and how best to manage it.

- Legal Troubles

    Employees who find themselves in trouble with the law will often have many concerns and ordeals with which neither the employer nor the union may be able to provide assistance. This includes situations such as criminal arrest, civil matters such as divorce and child custody battles, and domestic violence issues.

    If the matter is unrelated to their work, and the employee is available for work, i.e., not incarcerated or otherwise unable to attend work, representatives' involvement will be limited to managing the effects of these proceedings on the employees conduct in the workplace. Sometimes parties are able to work together to give the employee the space they need to deal with the situation, such as by arranging a leave of absence or temporary transfer. Representatives become more involved where the issue is related to some aspect of the employee's employment, such as when the criminal arrest was for stealing from the employer or the civil suit is the result of a workplace assault.

4.4 DISCIPLINE AND DISCHARGE

Employee discipline generally results from violation of some policy, rule or expectation established by the employer. The recognized and accepted purpose of discipline, in the labor relations context, is to encourage employees to correct unacceptable behavior or performance. It is not intended to be punitive.

Disciplinary action features prominently among the issues with which parties must deal because it has implications for the rights of employees and employers alike. Although discipline is a recognized right of management, the conditions under which discipline is imposed are generally appropriate for bargaining. Most collective bargaining agreements contain language addressing these issues, and breaches may be appealed through to arbitration. Among the factors typically negotiated are the parties' general philosophy regarding discipline; conditions under which discipline may be imposed; exceptions to the general provisions; and means for appealing discipline.

4.41 Coaching

Coaching, also referred to as counseling or coaching and counseling, is a precursor to formal disciplinary action. The intent behind coaching is to put the employee on notice that their conduct or performance is inconsistent with workplace standards and could have consequences if not corrected. Coaching is an important function for supervisors and may be done at any time. It may be formal or informal, written, oral or both, but should, ideally, be documented.

Coaching is not considered discipline, but it is an important element of corrective action. Ideally, coaching makes discipline unnecessary, but can provide a foundation it fail to bring about the required change.

4.42 Progressive Discipline

Most parties employ a progressive approach to discipline, which seeks to impose the least severe form of discipline that might be appropriate in the circumstances, and gives employees opportunities to demonstrate the desired change before advancing to more severe discipline. There is no hard-and-fast rule regarding the amount of time that must pass before further disciplinary action is taken. Rather, the nature of the issue and the specific circumstances will indicate when further discipline is appropriate.

Discipline may be escalated once there is sufficient evidence that the behavior has not been corrected. With some exceptions and variations, progressive discipline employs the following escalating actions:

1. *Verbal Warning:* This is the first and lowest level in the progressive discipline process. In practice, a verbal warning looks very much like coaching in that it must convey the same information to the employee and may be delivered orally, in writing or both. A major difference is that the employee is now told they are being disciplined, and are put on notice that they may be subject to further disciplinary action if there is a repeat of the

inappropriate conduct or if unsatisfactory performance has not sufficiently improved. A verbal warning should be documented and should note any previous coaching conducted and the results, if any, of those efforts.

2. *Written Reprimand:* This second level of discipline provides another opportunity for the employee to correct the issue before more stringent action is taken. It should cover the same ground as the verbal warning, and identify the prior corrective taken and the results, if any, of those efforts. Crucial to the effectiveness of the written reprimand is a clear admonition that the employee could be subject to more severe discipline should be conduct be repeated or performance continue to be unsatisfactory.

3. *Suspension*: Suspension is a form of temporary separation from employment during which the employee is removed from the workplace for a defined amount of time, and is not allowed to perform work on behalf of the employer. Suspensions may be imposed for as little as half a day up to the

maximum allowed by the parties' collective bargaining agreement or any other controlling rules. Except in rare cases, the employee does not receive compensation for the duration of the suspension. Their unpaid status may in turn result in further impacts, such as loss of vacation accruals, loss of overtime opportunities, or other benefits to which they otherwise would have had access.

4. *Demotion*: Demotion involves transferring the employee to a lower-level position with reduced pay. It is not always valid as a step in the progressive discipline process, but is a valuable alternative to termination where the issue driving the discipline is continued poor performance or conduct inappropriate for role the employee occupies.

5. *Termination*: An employee's expectation of continued employment rests strongly on their demonstrated willingness and ability to meet the employer's requirements. When this is absent ,following reasonable corrective efforts, termination may be the only option. Termination is sometimes referred to as "industrial capital punishment". Disciplinary

termination permanently revokes an employee's claim to all compensation, benefits and standing that came with the position, and may hamper their employment opportunities in the future. For these reasons, care should be taken to ensure termination is justified be it is implemented.

4.43 Exceptions to Progressive Discipline

While its merits are many, progressive discipline is not always the most appropriate response to an employee's failure to meet expectations. Progressive discipline is appropriate where there is reason to believe or expect that corrective action is likely to be effective and sufficient to protect the interests of others in the workplace. However, where situations indicate otherwise, appropriate disciplinary action may require departure from the progressive approach.

Skipping steps of the disciplinary process, such as going directly to a written warning or suspension on the first offense, will often be appropriate where the behavior is deemed correctable, but the action or its impact is so serious that lesser discipline is deemed inappropriate. Safety violations and certain forms of negligence may fall into this category. Conduct such as theft and violence may warrant the highest level of discipline, termination, for a first offense; it is not reasonable for an employer, or the employee's coworkers, to endure the significant negative impacts of such conduct before an employee may be removed from the workplace.

4.44 Zero-Tolerance Policies

Some parties establish zero-tolerance policies as part of their expectations or collective bargaining agreements. A zero-tolerance policy is generally understood to prescribe termination at the first occurrence of a particular offense, such as engaging in workplace violence or drug use. While such policies have their advantages, they can cause problems if they are poorly crafted or inconsistently applied.

Whether a zero-tolerance policy exists by the prerogative of management or by agreement with the union, parties should be crystal clear about what is meant by zero-tolerance, the specific rule or requirement to which it applies, to whom it applies, the conduct that will trigger disciplinary action, and what that action may be.

If the parties mean to make termination the only acceptable response to certain infractions, they must say so clearly in the policy. Polices which merely state that the employer or the parties have taken a position of zero-tolerance regarding certain conduct, but which go no further, establish only that the conduct will result in corrective action. Zero-tolerance under these terms may be equally demonstrated by imposition of a written reprimand as by termination. As a result, one decision-maker may view zero-tolerance as requiring termination, while another may view it simply as requiring some form of corrective action, which may include anything from coaching to termination. Where it may be shown that an employer has imposed varying degrees of discipline for violation of the same zero-tolerance policy, termination will not be held to be the only valid response.

4.5 Just Cause

The term *just cause*, also known as justifiable cause, reasonable cause, or sufficient cause, is used to denote a set of standards by which the appropriateness of disciplinary action may be assessed. The principle of just cause seeks to preserve and protect the rights of all parties to the labor-management relationship: the right of employees to know what is expected of them and to be treated fairly; the right of management to maintain order in the workplace and hold employees accountable; and the union's right to advocate on behalf of employees and protect their contractual rights.

Most practitioners are able to articulate the factors which determine just cause, but should be wary of approaching mechanically. The reality is that, while it requires certain material elements be present in order to prove its existence, just cause ultimately depends on a number of factors which may carry varying degrees of weight depending on the circumstances. The factors typically used to determine just cause are:

4.51 Reasonable Rule

The rule or policy on which the charge is based should be reasonable and related to work, the employee's responsibilities, or the employer's protected interests.

4.52 Prior Notice of the Rules and Consequences

Notice of rules or standards on which discipline is based may take various forms and may be accomplished in a variety of ways, most commonly by the setting and restating of expectations, training, and prior disciplinary action.

The employee must also have been aware of the potential consequences for breaching the rules.

An exception to this requirement is recognized where a rule is or should be obvious to a reasonable person, such as that theft is unacceptable. In such cases, knowledge of both the expectation and the consequence is imputed to the employee, and an employer is not required to prove it provided specific notice before imposing discipline.

4.53 Proof of Wrongdoing

There must be sufficient proof or evidence the employee actually engaged in the conduct or was responsible for the issues for which he is being disciplined. If the employee's guilt cannot be established there may not be just cause for discipline.

4.54 Fair and Thorough Investigation

Investigations are the most common means by which employers establish proof of wrongdoing. Investigations performed for purposes of establishing whether the employee is indeed culpable of the offense for which they may be facing discipline must be fair and thorough. Inadequate, biased or superficial investigation generally will not be sufficient to support just cause.

4.55   Due Process

In the context of disciplinary action, due process requires the preservation and performance of the rights of employees facing disciplinary action. The extent and form of due process required varies to some extent depending on the nature of the infraction and the particular environment in which the employer operates, but will generally include the following elements:

- Right to Representation

    Employees are entitled to have a representative of their choosing during disciplinary procedures if they so desire. While, in the context of the labor-management relationship, the union will be the assumed representative, the employee retains the right to choose who will represent him in disciplinary proceedings. Some employees choose to be represented by an attorney, and yet others opt to have a friend or family member present for moral support. Parties should not attempt to interfere with these choices.

    Employees may request, and should be allowed, representation at any stage of the process, including at investigation interviews and Loudermill hearings. Denying an employee representation is to deny them their due process rights. *NLRB v. J. Weingarten, Inc.*, 420 U.S. 251 (1975) established employees' right to have a representative present during any meeting with management they believe is likely to result in disciplinary action.

Case law has vacillated over the years as to whether Weingarten rights apply only in the private sector or also in the public sector, and whether the right must be affirmatively granted to or appropriated by the employee. More often than not, parties will have articulated their expectations with regard to union representation in the collective bargaining agreement. Some parties require management to proactively notify employees of their rights when embarking on investigations or other disciplinary actions, while others merely require it be granted upon the employee's request.

- Notice of the Charge
  Employees have a right to be informed of the reason they are being disciplined, the specific

conduct leading to the discipline, and rules on which the discipline is based.

- Opportunity to Respond

    Employees in the public sector, in particular, have additional due process protections which are rooted in the fourteenth amendment to the American constitution. Under that amendment, the government, as the employer, may not deprive individuals of their property rights without due process. Government employees who have attained standing with the employer have a property interest in their jobs, and in the pay and benefits they provide. Any disciplinary action that will effectively deprive an employee of some or all of their property interests may not occur unless and until the employee has been given notice of the charges, the intended action, and an opportunity to respond. Suspension of any length, demotion, and termination will all require this due process requirement be met.

    These due process rights were codified in *Cleveland Board of Education v. Loudermill, 470 U.S. 532 (1985)*, which granted public sector employees the right to a hearing before certain discipline could be imposed. Known as a

Loudermill hearing, this opportunity to respond may take the form of a formalized meeting or hearing, or by written response made by the employee. The purpose of a Loudermill hearing is to give the employee an opportunity to provide any information they believe is important for the decision maker to have before imposing discipline. This may include mitigating information, input from others or further feedback from the employee. The decision-maker retains discretion as to whether to impose the same or a different level of discipline as originally contemplated, or no discipline at all. Employees may choose to waive their Loudermill rights, but parties should require such waivers to be in writing.

4.56 Equitable Treatment

Fairness in the imposition of discipline across the bargaining unit, workgroup or organization is a critical element of just cause. Uneven or arbitrary disciplinary action undermines an employer's ability to establish that action taken in a particular case was not capricious or discriminatory in nature. In addition, the rule or policy upon which the discipline is based must be shown to have been consistently enforced. Where an employer has previously not disciplined employees for breaching a rule or policy, it will be difficult to defend subsequent action unless employees had been expressly notified that discipline will, from that point forward, be meted out for infraction of the policy.

4.57 Appropriate Level of Discipline

The discipline imposed should be commensurate with the infraction. In other words, the punishment needs to fit the crime. Termination at a first offense of massive embezzlement will likely be found to be justifiable, but the same response for miscalculation of the petty-cash balance will not.

4.58 Mitigating and Aggravating Factors

Mitigating factors are those which indicate lesser or no discipline may be warranted. Among them are length of service, lack of prior discipline or evidence the conduct was inadvertent or accidental. Management inaction, such as where a supervisor failed to take appropriate action to arrest or correct the conduct, or to do so in a timely manner may also be a mitigating factor.

Aggravating factors are those which strongly support the imposition of discipline, and/or indicate more severe discipline may warranted. They include factors such as length of service, significant disciplinary history or willful negligence.

Notice that length of service may be mitigating or aggravating, depending on the circumstances: A long-time employee may be granted clemency because of his years of unblemished service, but may also be dealt with more harshly precisely because of their depth of knowledge of the workplace standards and expectations. Conversely, a newer employee might obtain leniency because they could not be held to have the same depth of understanding of the expectations, but their brief track record may serve to exacerbate the seriousness of certain misconduct.

Note that certain just-cause elements may themselves be mitigating or aggravating factors. Issues such as lack of proper notice of a rule, or the significance of the rule within the workplace may indicate lesser or more severe discipline is warranted. It is unusual for a single factor to drive a disciplinary decision; in most cases, the appropriateness of a disciplinary action will be the result of determining the relative weight of all applicable factors given the specific circumstances.

4.6 LAST CHANCE AGREEMENTS

A last-chance agreement is an individual contract between an employee and the employer which redefines the terms of their employment following, or in lieu of, severe disciplinary action. The employee is expected to comply with the terms of the last chance agreement, on pain of termination. A last chance agreement may be proffered by the employer or the union, and either may decline to enter into such an agreement. However, once it has been agreed to, the last chance agreement becomes a negotiated instrument between the employer and employee.

Last chance agreements are most commonly used in circumstances involving matter such as substance abuse, workplace violence, and persistent unsatisfactory performance or conduct. They provide employees with further opportunities to meet the employer's expectations where they would otherwise have been separated from employment.

These agreements are highly fact-specific and will incorporate terms intended to curb the behavior for which the employee would have been terminated. Before entering into a last chance agreement, parties should determine what are the critical goals of the agreement, the likelihood the employee will be able to meet the required terms, and how breaches will be addressed.

Last-chance agrees should be used sparingly. When properly crafted and enforced, they are effective tools for changing employee behavior and safeguarding the employer's interests. They also benefit the employee, by allowing them to retain employment and demonstrate their ability and willingness to meet expectations. However, when a last chance agreement is poorly crafted, contains unfair or unattainable conditions, or is not enforced by the employer as prescribed in the agreement, it loses its effectiveness and may ultimately prove counterproductive.

Chapter 5
Labor-Management Relations in Operations

It is an accepted truism that no two parties can hope to regulate every aspect of their relationship in any written document; in the final analysis, the good faith of the contracting parties, and their respective willingness to establish a workable relationship, is the controlling factor.

Zack, Bloch, Labor Agreement in Negotiation and Arbitration, 1983

There are few aspects of an entity's operation, or a worker's employment, that remain untouched by the labor-management relationship. In fact, it is in the daily activities of the workplace and the ongoing interaction between management and labor that most collective bargaining occurs.

In a very real way, the labor-management relationship is defined and redefined by the conduct of the parties in their day-to-day operations. This is where the proverbial rubber meets the road. The number and scope of issues that may arise during a typical workday is practically unlimited. So, too, are the opportunities for parties to put the labor-management relationship to its best use, characterized by collaboration, respect for the rights of the other, and commitment to resolving issues. Labor relations professionals must be prepared to play multiple roles according to the types of issue s that arise and the demands of the working environment, to provide guidance and support. Ideally, the practitioner is able to spot potential problems early and identify workable solutions to meet the needs of the workplace.

This chapter addresses some of the most common ways collective bargaining occurs within — and affects — the workplace, on a daily basis.

5.1 LABOR MANAGEMENT COMMITTEES

Ongoing collaboration is a feature of a healthy labor-management relationship. One way in which management and labor collaborate on workplace matters is through the use of *labor-management committees,* or LMCs. A labor-management committee facilitates targeted or ongoing collaboration and problem-solving between the employer and the union. Many operational matters are appropriate for this forum, and LMCs can be particularly effective in helping parties develop and maintain a productive working relationship.

5.11 Purpose of LMCs

Labor-management committees are usually established within specific workgroups or bargaining units, with a view to addressing the needs and concerns of that particular group. They generally involve regular meetings of representatives from management, the union, and employee groups. They may be established as an ongoing forum for addressing issues of concern, or for a specific purpose, such as implementation of new technology or a move to a new location.

Labor-management committees are particularly useful where employee input is needed or may be valuable in making decisions that will affect them. The union's involvement ensures the interests of the whole bargaining unit can be represented, and management can obtain input from and share information with employees without the risk of direct dealing.

5.12 Benefits of LMCs

Labor-management committees not only support, but may also bring the added benefit of advancing the labor-management relationship by improving mutual understanding and trust among employees, members of management and labor. Because they require parties to share information, the likelihood of one party being met with unpleasant surprises (at least regarding any issue addressed by the LMC) is greatly reduced, and opportunities for identifying and resolving issues quickly and effectively are greatly increased. In addition, participants may obtain other benefits: management and union representatives learn to interact and work with each other in a more productive manner, and employees are better able to be heard by the their management and to appreciate the needs and interests of the employer.

5.13 Requirements for Effective LMCs

Parties can help to ensure the effectiveness and success of labor-management committees by including the following elements:

- A Clear Charter

  Parties must be clear as to the purpose for which the committee has been established, the desired goals and outcomes, and the manner in which the committee will be conducted. Ideally, the LMC charter is a product of discussion between representatives of management and the union.

- Right Participants

    Committee members must include representatives from management, the union and the affected employee group(s). Management selects the individuals who will represent its interests and the union selects employees who will represent the interests of the groups of which they are a part. Parties will often attempt to ensure a workable balance of management and labor representatives and, for ongoing labor-management committees, may agree to a service period and rules for rotating employee participants.

- Information Sharing

    This is critical to the successful functioning of a labor-management committee. Parties must be willing to exchange such information as will inform the committee's efforts and guide decision making.

    The parties may agree to rules for confidentiality as needed, but it is important to remember that one function of the committee is to ensure information is properly disseminated throughout the bargaining unit, so the need for confidentiality must be balanced with the need for and benefits of communicating directly with the employees. Employee representatives are usually charged with this responsibility, and will also often bring information back to the committee regarding employees' thoughts and reactions to issues being discussed. Similarly, management representatives are able to shuttle information between the committee and company leadership that may help guide decision-making.

5.2 JOB CLASSIFICATION

Job classification is a method by which the characteristics that separate one body of work from another are identified and defined. A *body of work* is a set of tasks and responsibilities typically performed by a single worker. It is assumed to be a discrete, quantifiable unit. A job classification will often be documented in the form of a job description, which lists the characteristics that separate one body of work from another, its purpose, critical functions and required skillsets.

Job classifications are objective constructs, and are not affected by the performance or qualifications of any individual who occupies the classification. Although most job classifications are carefully documented and formally established, this is not always the case. Employees may perform work under a shared job title and rate of pay but have no formalized classification. Even in such situations, it is always possible to identify the predominant characteristics of the work being performed.

Job classification is its own discipline, and often employs complex analyses to establish what makes up a body of work, what requirements are necessary and reasonable, and how it fits within the larger classification and compensation structure of the organization.

While labor relations professionals will not necessarily be tasked with creating or managing job classifications, most will be required, at some point, to provide guidance and input regarding new classifications or changes to existing classifications. This is because, within the labor relations context, job classification plays a major role in establishing critical boundaries for a bargaining unit, since parties rely on job classification as an objective framework for determining the responsibilities and remuneration that should be attached to a body of work.

5.21 Mis-classification

Mis-classification of employees, or of the body of work they perform, occurs when an employee occupies a job classification that is notably different from the body of work they actually perform. This is a fairly common occurrence. Mis-classification often results from a gradual accretion or degression of duties, operational changes or mismatch with an employee's skills or qualifications which results in assignment of work more suited to the employee's abilities. Mis-classification can go unnoticed for extended periods of time. In many cases, it will not significantly impact on the workplace, but under certain circumstances, it can cause major difficulties for the labor and management, such as during organizing efforts and when bodies of work are created or changed.

- <u>Organizing & Defining Bargaining Units</u>

    One of the first and most important elements of an organizing effort is determining the appropriate bargaining unit. Recall that a bargaining unit is made up of employees who share a community of interests, largely determined by shared employment circumstances and similar claims to pay and other benefits.

Employees who occupy the same job classification generally perform the same type of work, under the same working conditions. They must have the same or similar qualifications, and are expected meet the same requirements and standards of performance. In addition, the manner in which they are compensated is generally the same. For all these reasons, the job classification often is the first place parties look to identify employees who should belong to a particular bargaining unit.

Proper classification of bodies of work, and of potential employee members, is important in organizing because only those employees who may legitimately be part of the bargaining unit may cast a valid vote for representation.

When bodies of work are misclassified, or employees occupy the wrong job classification, simply identifying the employees assigned to a particular job classification may not be quite as reliable for purposes of establishing who should be included in the bargaining unit. In order to ensure a valid election, and an appropriate bargaining unit, parties often need to conduct a careful review of the work actually being performed by potential bargaining unit members to ensure the correct employees will be included and, just as importantly, that none are inadvertently left out.

There are functions and responsibilities which will preclude some employees from union representation.

- *Supervisors:* In many states, individuals with supervisory responsibilities are excluded from union representation, or must belong to a separate bargaining unit from those they supervise. During an organizing effort, management may attempt to have certain employees excluded because of their supervisory status, while the union may insist on their inclusion on the basis that the work they perform is appropriate for representation. Questions regarding supervisory status are often not as easy to resolve as might be assumed, even if an employee occupies a job clarification with the word supervisor or manager in the title.

  In the labor relations context, an employee is a supervisor if, in addition to overseeing and directing the daily work of employees, they have the authority to hire, to fire and to discipline those employees. In many organizations, employees may hold the title of supervisor and be responsible for monitoring and managing work, but may not have decision-making authority. These employees will gently not be exclude from union representation.

It should be noted that standards regarding classification of employees as supervisors tend to be more stringent in the public sector, with the result that fewer persons performing supervisory roles in the public sector are allowed to organize than might be the case in the private sector.

True supervisors, in this sense, have the ability to impact the employment of the employees they supervise. Within a represented group, this creates a conflict of interest for supervisory employees, because their primary role is to act in the interest of the employer by managing resources and time, keeping order and even administering discipline. This inherent conflict is the reason many states make supervisors ineligible for representation by a union.

- *Confidential Employees:* Individuals who, as part of their normal duties, handle or are privy to confidential information regarding negotiations between the parties, are also excluded from union representation. Because of this, it is possible to have certain positions within a represented job classification that are designated a non-represented positions.

Review of job classification for the purposes of determining the appropriate composition of the bargaining will generally involve two separate but related approaches. First, parties will want to confirm that the work intended or understood to be performed within a particular job classification is both appropriate for representation and consistent with the work for which representation is intended. Second, they will need to verify that the employees occupying the classification are actually performing the work of that classification.

5.22 Unit Clarification

Disputes as to whether bodies of work or employees are properly classified for purposes of establishing a bargaining unit may be resolved via *unit clarification*. Unit clarification is a process administered by an oversight agency upon request filed by either or both parties to the dispute which uses the factors described above to determine which employees rightly belong in a defined bargaining unit.

5.23 New and Changing Bodies of Work

Parties often negotiate the impact of classification changes and additions to address their effect on employees' *standing* within the bargaining unit, i.e., whether an employee has a legitimate claim to the position and the negotiated benefits that come with it. Standing is usually attained after an employee has completed any required probationary periods or other qualifying standards. Factors such as employees' seniority in the new classification, when and how standing is attained, how compensation changes will be implemented and how they should be treated for purposes of layoff and recall are important considerations when classification changes are implemented.

Because a job classification is part of a larger organizational system, changes to existing classifications should not be considered in isolation. Employers and unions must assess how planned changes might affect other classifications and the employees who occupy those classifications.

- New Job Classifications
When a new body of work is established, the

factors that determine how that work is classified will also determine whether it will belong to an existing bargaining unit. As we shall soon see, the mere similarity of a particular body of work to others in a bargaining unit may not be sufficient to establish that the work necessarily belong to that bargaining unit.

While some new classifications may be added to a bargaining unit based on the work itself, new work may also be accreted to a bargaining unit by agreement of the parties. For example, if a collective bargaining agreement states that the union is the exclusive representative of all employees engaged in a specific function within the organization, any new positions the employer creates to perform that function will be added to the bargaining unit.

- <u>New Positions Within a Job Classification</u>
New positions within an existing job classification will belong to the same bargaining unit as other existing positions in that classification, unless subject to a specific carve-out, such as an administrative assistant position which will have confidential responsibilities.

- Changes to Job Classifications

    Job classifications are generally treated as static once defined, but they are mutable. Over the course of time, classifications may change as the manner and environment in which the work is performed change. One obvious cause of such change is technology, but they may also be affected by evolving regulatory requirements, operational needs, changes in the size and composition of the workforce, geographical considerations, and other factors. When such changes occur, parties should ensure classifications are kept up to date, and that incumbents are still properly classified.

    It is possible for certain tasks and requirements to change without impacting the job classification to a significant degree. However, some changes are more significant, resulting in different qualification requirements, different levels of responsibility and even changes in compensation. In some instances, reclassification may result in bodies of work moving into or out of a bargaining unit, an impact that will always require negotiation.

5.24 Bargaining Job Classifications

Determining the work to be performed is one of the rights normally reserved to management, and the employer generally may also unilaterally determine what work should be added, what needs to be changed and what bodies of work to eliminate. Once a new job classification is created, if the body of work is a non-represented body of work, i.e., it does not fit in any classification or work grouping represented by an existing bargaining unit, management is free to set pay and other standards unilaterally as well. If, however, the body of work is congruent with other classifications in a bargaining unit, it will be necessary to negotiate pay and other working conditions.

Parties may also need to bargain over impacts to other represented classifications affected by the classification at issue, such as, for example, when a new classification begins performing a portion of the work historically done by another classification. Parties will need to discuss the extent to which the original classification might be impacted: will those tasks be taken away completely, or will they be shared between the classifications? Will incumbents retain full-time work, or will their roles be so diminished as to result in less than full-time positions? How will the removal or addition of tasks affect the qualifications required? Will pay need to be adjusted? Parties will often seek input from classifications experts to help determine the extent to which a new classification, or a change to an existing classification, will impact either the classification itself or others related to it. The extent to which parties must negotiate such changes will depend, as always, on the nature of the change and its impacts.

5.25 Jurisdictional Issues

New and changing job classifications affect not only bargaining unit composition, but may also affect the union's *jurisdiction*. The term jurisdiction is used to denote a union's legitimate claim to a body of work.

Jurisdictional issues can arise where there is more than one union in the workplace, and particularly where there is some overlap or similarity in the work performed by the different bargaining units, but they may also be concerned with whether a particular body of work should be represented at all. Jurisdictional issues may be resolved by analyzing certain aspects of the work to determine its appropriate placement within the organization.

- The critical tasks and responsibilities of the classification

  It is important to determine whether the tasks in question are germane to a classification that has been recognized as belonging to a particular bargaining unit. Tasks and responsibilities which represent the essential functions of a job, that is, the central purpose for which the job exists, are often the first indicators of a job's proper classification and whether it belongs in a particular bargaining unit. If the essential tasks are the same as those for which a union has already been certified as the representative, it is likely that work will belong to that union. If the tasks in question are not characteristic of the essential tasks of a represented classification the job likely will not be considered to be within the exclusive jurisdiction of the union representing the bargaining unit.

- The amount of time spent performing the essential functions

  Occasional performance, or performance for short periods of time, of a task deemed essential to another classification will not make that body of work subject to the other classification. However, if a task is being performed on a regular, ongoing basis by an employee in a different classification, or if they spend significant portions of their workday performing those tasks, this likely will indicate that the work belongs in a different classification or bargaining unit.

- <u>Whether specialized training or knowledge is required:</u> The degree to which a task which requires specialized knowledge, training, or other qualification may help determine whether the task should be considered to belong exclusively to a particular job classification. Tasks which require no specialized training or skill, such as general administrative duties or driving, are not determinative of classification or jurisdiction.

- <u>Location and Means of Performance</u>
The location where the work is performed may also affect jurisdiction. A body of work that has been represented by a union for years at a particular location, for example, will likely remain under the jurisdiction of that union. However, the same body of work, created at a different location, may not necessarily accrue to that union. This is so because employees at the new location may not share a community of

interests with employees at the original location because working conditions are strikingly different, or because a different union has jurisdiction over all employees at the new location.

- <u>Bargaining History</u>

    The length of time a body of work has been under the exclusive jurisdiction of a union may also be a factor. If a classification has been represented by a union for only a short time, it will be difficult for that union to claim jurisdiction if a different union has represented the classification for an extended period of time.

    Although most jurisdictional issues will not be resolved by applying only one of these factors, not all of them will be relevant in all cases. Most situations require identification and balancing of all relevant factors in order to reach the most appropriate conclusion.

5.3 COMPENSABLE TIME

The term *compensable time* is any time for which employees are entitled to receive pay. Compensable time does not only include an employee's regular working hours, but all time during which employees are required to be engaged for the employer's benefit or at the employer's direction.

Applying this standard, it is generally easy to identify what time is compensable to an employee. However, there are scenarios under which compensability is not quite so clear. These are typically situations in which the employee is engaged in activity that may or may not be directly related to their jobs, but which may occur within or adjacent to the employee's working hours. Situations such as emergency personnel who must remain available to respond as needed during their assigned lunch breaks are good examples of circumstances in which an employee may not be entitled to pay even though they are not actively performing work activities.

Jobs for which employees must wear or carry certain equipment or protective gear may require more than nominal amounts of time to put on and remove. Case law has been firmly established for some time that these activities are compensable where they are an inherent part of the work to be performed and may not be separated from the rest of the work without hazard to employees' health and safety, or their ability to perform required tasks. Examples include hazmat and some types of construction work.

Where a job necessarily exposes employees to contaminants, or where employees are required to clean equipment and other gear after performing certain tasks or at the end of the workday, the time spent performing those activities will be compensable. As with donning and doffing, these tasks are considered inextricably tied to the performance of the work. Parties generally will either agree that employees perform these tasks within their normal working hours or provide additional pay for time spent performing these activities.

5.4 NON-COMPENSABLE AND UNPAID TIME

In addition to defining the workday and workweek for employees in the bargaining unit, and activities for which employees will be compensated, parties will often also specify time periods during the workday for which employees are not paid. This is unencumbered time during which employees may not be expected or required to be actively engaged in work activities. Workers are completely relieved of duty and may pursue their own interests without restriction.

5.41 Rest and Meal Breaks

Unencumbered time during the workday generally includes rest and breaks. Break times are intended to provide employees with a period of rest and refreshment to support their ability to function effectively throughout the day. Most states set minimum standards for break and mealtimes for all employees. Parties are free to agree to more generous standards, but may not negotiate away these requirements unless specifically provided for by statute.

Because breaks and meals are unencumbered time for the employee, they are typically unpaid. In some sectors, parties are able to negotiate working meal periods during which employees are not completely released from duty but may be required to remain available to work if needed. This is sometimes the case in law enforcement and some other safety-sensitive positions. In such circumstances, the break is not unencumbered and the employee will be entitled to some amount of compensation for that time.

5.42 Off-Duty Hours

Unencumbered time also includes those periods of time outside of an employee's scheduled working hours. Generally speaking, the time following the end of one shift and prior to the start of the next shift is unencumbered time for the employee: they are fully released from duty, there is no expectation of performance and they may devote that time to their own interests and benefits without restriction. Whenever the employer interrupts or curtails this unencumbered time, some form of compensation will be due.

5.43 Commute Time

The time an employee spends traveling to and from work is generally not considered to be compensable. This is so because, although the commute is necessary in order for the employee to get to work, they are not actively engaged in the work during the commute. Employees also have discretion as to the manner in which they commute and, to a great extent, the amount of time they spend commuting. The employer does not control the employee's commute and therefore is not obligated to compensate them for that time.

Traditionally, exceptions to these rules were the result of assignment to remote locations, travel to other worksites during the workday, or travel time to alternative work locations outside of normal working hours. More recently, employers have agreed to compensate employees for time spent performing work during a commute using remote technology. Even here, the employee is not being compensated for commuting, per se, but for actively performing tasks recognized to be for the employer's benefit.

5.5 WORKING HOURS

Working hours, one of the subjects over which management and labor are required to negotiate, can be one of the most complex areas for practitioners to manage. Because it is a mandatory subject of bargaining, setting and changing employees' schedules and working hours often requires parties to spend significant time bargaining related matters.

This is an area in which external law bears heavily on the labor-management relationship. While parties are free to make agreements regarding working hours, none of those agreements may run afoul of existing federal or state laws.

5.51 Setting and Changing Working Hours

When negotiating working hours, management will seek to ensure its operational and staffing needs can be met and labor will seek to ensure employees are not subjected to excessive, onerous or unfavorable working schedules. Parties seek to balance these interests in negotiations to help regulate working schedules and reduce uncertainty.

Because working hours may need to change occasionally to accommodate business or other needs, and because work sometimes must occur outside of what are generally considered to be normal working hours, parties often negotiate language into their contracts to guide the manner in which such changes must be implemented, and to effect any related changes to pay or other benefits. Language such as this eliminates the need to return to the bargaining table for each instance in which employees' working hours might need to be adjusted.

This type of language is sometimes viewed as an agreed waiver of bargaining but, by establishing terms that will be applied in certain circumstances, the parties have not waived bargaining. Rather, they have simply negotiated the changes in advance. The most common expressions of this type of scenario are:

- Schedule Changes
  Collective bargaining agreements often set parameters for changing employees' schedules, such as providing for advance notice of changes

or placing restrictions on when employees may be moved from one schedule to another. These restrictions are intended to guard against changes that will deprive employees of a sufficient break in service, or of the time needed to adjust to a new schedule. Some contracts include what are essentially monetary penalties to the employer, additional monies that must be paid to the employee, in the event the stated requirements are not met for implementing a change of schedule.

- Shift Changes

  Shift change language may be general or specific, depending on the nature of the work and the frequency with which such changes are expected. It will almost always provide a premium for employees when their shifts are to be changed at the request of management. The premium is intended to compensate employees for the disruption in their work/life routines and provide an incentive to preserve stable and predictable working hours for employees.

5.52 Overtime

Overtime is typically defined as time worked in excess of the normal workday or workweek.

Overtime may occur as a *shift extension*, where the extra work time effectively extends the normal workday, such as when an employee is asked to continue working beyond their usual end time to complete a task or assignment. Overtime may also arise from an assignment of work outside of the employee's normal work schedule, such as being asked to work on a scheduled day off or holiday. Overtime assignments may be mandatory or voluntary.

Overtime is typically paid at a premium rate, usually at one and a half or two times the employee's normal rate of pay, but may also be higher or paid at straight time (the employee's normal rate of pay). Employee's may be compensated for working overtime with additional leave time rather than by actual wages, at a multiplier equal to what they otherwise would have been paid. This is known as *compensatory* (or *comp*) time. It has historically been most prominent in the public sector but today is widely used in the private sector as well.

When overtime occurs regularly, it may be assigned on a rotational basis to all eligible employees. This is done to avoid placing too heavy a burden on a few employees. Overtime rotation helps prevent employee burnout which can ultimately compromise employees' health and safety in the workplace. It also prevents granting an unfair advantage to a few who receive large amounts of overtime pay as compared with others.

5.53 Call-Back & Emergency Response

A call-back occurs when employees are asked to return to the workplace following completion of their shift, or prior to the usual start of their shift, due to some unforeseen circumstance. In these situations, neither the employee's shift nor their schedule has been changed, but they are required to perform work outside of their normal working hours for some period of time.

In times past, call-back was understood to occur when the employee had physically left the workplace and was required to return the workplace or another assigned work location to perform work. Today, most call-back language accommodates scenarios in which employees need not report to a specific location in order to perform the necessary work, allowing for call-back to be performed via telephone or by logging on to a work-related computer system. In these cases, compensation is figured from the time the employee responds to a call or logs into a system, rather than when they leave for or arrive at a physical location.

Most contracts provide additional pay for employees providing this type of response, the intent being to compensate them for the inconvenience of having to work during a time they should have been free of duty. Some contracts provide a minimum amount of pay for responding employees (e.g. a minimum of two hours of pay, regardless of the amount of time actually needed to complete the work), and may also prescribe pay at a premium rate, such as at the overtime rate, for the time spent working. For situations in which the call-back results in employees continuing to work up to and beyond the beginning of their usual shift, any premium pay provided usually ends at the time the normal shift begins.

5.6   LEAVES

Leaves are a form of unencumbered time for which employees may be entitled to receive pay. The types of leaves available to employees today vary greatly, and many are required by statute.

The conditions under which employees may be eligible for leave, how much leave will be granted, and other requirements such as whether and when they may be paid or unpaid will generally be prescribed in the governing legal standards or, at the organizational level, the policies that have been established by the employer or negotiated in the collective bargaining agreement.

Vacation and sick leave are two of the most common types of leave negotiated by parties to a collective bargaining agreement. Even when vacation or sick time is paid, it must be treated as unencumbered time to the employee. Any interruption in this time will require some compensation, either in the form of a premium payment or as regular pay rather than a charge against the employee's leave entitlement.

5.7 SAFETY

Employers are required by law, and by conscience, to provide a safe and healthful working environment for all employees. Certainly, there are legal and regulatory standards that come to bear on every workplace, regardless of whether the employer is party to a labor-management relationship. However, because safety is so important to employees' well-being in the workplace, it is often considered a shared responsibility of management and employees.

Workers' ability to perform their jobs in the safest possible manner, and the impacts of their inability or failure to do so, is closely tied to both management's and employees' interests. For these reasons, the area of safety and health is one which lends itself to productive, ongoing collaboration between labor and management.

Jobs which have been classified as safety-sensitive positions often require additional negotiation between parties to establish the conditions under which employees will perform their responsibilities. Safety-sensitive positions include those for which the work is inherently hazardous, such as firefighting and long-haul truck driving, but also those that may expose worker to hazardous conditions.

Parties will generally negotiate such conditions of employment for these roles such as maintaining certifications, drug testing procedures and provision and use of personal protective equipment (PPE).

5.71 Personal Protective Equipment (PPE)

PPE required for any represented position is a mandatory subject of bargaining, since it ultimately is a form of benefits or wages.

The type of equipment employees must have, the quantity and quality of such equipment, when they must be used and when they should be replaced are all issues that management and labor may bargain over. The question of cost, and of who should be responsible for those costs, is an important one.

In most cases, management will bear the cost of all required PPE. However, some parties agree to varying terms based the type of PPE and the degree to which it is required to perform the work. Items of PPE that are more personal in nature, and which may not generally be used by more than one person, PPE that may be used in other contexts or which is optional, are sometimes only covered by the employer to a limited extent, if at all. Employees will be responsible for costs incurred beyond the provided amount.

5.8 WORK RULES, POLICIES AND CHANGES

Employers may establish policies which exist independent of the collective bargaining agreement. Employer policies address wide-ranging, organizational matters that affect employees and/or the way in which they do their work. Bargaining unit employees are not exempt from employer policies unless either the contract or the policy expressly excludes them. Therefore, bargaining unit employees are often expected to adhere to workplace policies just as other employees are.

As always, whether and to what extent the employer is required to negotiate its policies depends on its relative significance to either management's or employees' core interests. Policies regarding issues deemed to be within management's rights may be implemented without bargaining on the decisions.

Work rules is a term used for any workplace policies, guidelines, rules or procedures that relate to how employees perform their responsibilities, how performance is measured, how they conduct themselves in the workplace, and how any rewards or sanctions will apply.

Work rules are generally set by the employer, with or without some degree of negotiation between the parties. Whether a work rule must be negotiated before being established and implemented depends, as we have previously seen, on the degree to which the rule, or its effects, implicate either employees' essential employment interests, or management's reserved rights.

Work rules generally go further than general contract language, specifying the manner in which the provisions of the contract will be administered on a practical, day to day level. Generally speaking, their purpose is to establish expectations, standards and guidelines that apply to covered employees. Work rules cover everything from PPE requirements to overtime assignment, to prohibited shop floor conduct.

The type, number and extent of work rules in force in a particular workplace at any time is highly dependent on the nature of the working environment and the requirements of the work being performed. Some work rules become part of the collective bargaining agreement, either by actually being incorporated into the contract, or by implication as the parties exhibit mutual reliance on the rules and work together to set and change standards.

Some of the most common types of work rules negotiated between parties include:

- Timekeeping
  Work rules related to timekeeping address how negotiated wages and working hours language is administered by the employer and exercised by employees on a day-to-day basis. Timekeeping rules often spell out requirements for clocking in and out of shifts; requesting time off; changing and exchanging shifts; late arrivals and early departure; breaks; timesheet completion and submission, and more.

- Attendance

    Attendance management seeks to ensure the availability of a sufficient workforce, both in terms of quantity and quality, to meet operational needs on an ongoing basis. Because attendance is, in essence, most closely related to employers' interests in the methods and means of production, it is not necessarily a mandatory subject of bargaining, and employers may determine the standards and requirements for employees' attendance. However, because it often touches on some employee rights and benefits, and may ultimately impact employees' employment status, it is an area in which collaboration or negotiation of the impacts of the policy or work rules is beneficial.

- Overtime

    To ensure the parties' goals and expectations regarding the use, distribution and compensation of overtime work are consistently achieved, detailed guidelines will often be agreed to by the parties. Work rules related to overtime cover such issues as who decides whether overtime is needed; how it will be assigned and to whom (many workplaces use a rotational model); whether and how mandatory overtime will be used; and guidelines for meeting overtime needs in emergency situations.

5.81 Changes to Work Rules and Policies

Whether bargaining on changes to work rule or policies is required, and the extent to which bargaining is required, will, as always, depend on the nature of the change. Representatives should keep in mind that changes to a rule or policy that was previously bargained will generally require bargaining before those changes can be implemented. Rules or policies that were implemented without bargaining may require bargaining if the change involves a mandatory subject of bargaining, or the impact to employees is significant.

Chapter 6
Labor-Management Relations in Conflict

The true strength of the dispute settlement machinery in collective bargaining is its emphasis on the joint resolution of a dispute at the earlier steps...
Zack, A., *A Handbook for Grievance Arbitration: Procedural & Ethical Issues*, (1992)

Even with the best efforts of the parties, conflicts will inevitably occur over the course of the labor-management relationship. They will arise during the formation of a bargaining unit, in the process of contract negotiations, in managing employee issues, in the day-to-day operations and in the interactions between labor and management representatives and their constituents.

Conflict does not only occur because of either party's inappropriate actions, but can also be the natural outgrowth of legitimate collective bargaining activity, such as appealing disciplinary action or providing notification of undesirable operational changes.

Collective bargaining obligations do not cease when there is conflict. Conflict resolution is an essential component of collective bargaining. In fact, the collective bargaining system is uniquely suited to the resolution of workplace disputes, because it was developed for the express purpose of managing the types of conflict parties typically encounter.

It is important for practitioners to have confidence in the collective bargaining process and develop the ability to guide constituents through conflict in a manner that honors the labor-management relationship.

6.1 Approach to Resolving Conflicts

Labor relations professionals are, in a real sense, conflict management experts: they are responsible for the strategy, response to, and resolution of, any variety and number of conflicts. At times, they may even have the ability to prevent or alleviate conflict.

There is often more than one appropriate way to respond to a conflict, but any approach parties choose must be taken with a view to preserving the relationship. Representatives should consider the critical facts of the situation; identify the problem to be solved or issue to be addressed; determine whether or how its potential impacts; consider what needs to be done to protect their constituents' rights and interests; consider the rights of the other party; and determine what tool(s) would best accomplish their goals.

6.2 GRIEVANCES

A grievance is a dispute resolution mechanism for unions and employers who are parties to a collective bargaining agreement. It is the most common tool used to deal with conflict in the labor-management relationship.

In broad terms, a grievance is an allegation that one of the parties has violated the collective bargaining agreement. The manner in which the parties define the grievance sets the scope of issues for which the grievance procedure may be used. Any provision within the contract will be a viable subject for grievance, unless expressly excluded by agreement of the parties. Exclusions to the grievance procedure are few, but must be clearly stated in the collective bargaining agreement to be recognized as an exception.

It is important to not that not all conflicts that arise within the labor-management relationship are true grievances, even though they may need to be addressed within the collective bargaining framework. Distinguishing between legitimate grievances and other types of complaints makes it possible to respond appropriately in different situations.

- Gripes

    A gripe is an issue that legitimately affects represented employees but which does not implicate any provision of the contract. The term is not intended to convey that such concerns are trivial or unimportant. They often are legitimate issues, but ones for which resort to the contract is not an option, either because they are not addressed in the collective bargaining agreement or involve a matter over which the parties are not obligated or allowed to being. Such complaints cannot be resolved using the grievance process and must be addressed by other means.

- Unfair Labor Practice Claims (ULPs)

    As was previously discussed, a ULP arises from a violation of, or a failure to meet, statutory bargaining obligations. They do not derive from contractual terms created by agreement of the parties.

Some collective bargaining activities may implicate both the negotiated contract language and legal obligations, such as a requirement to negotiate the impacts of certain workplace changes. In such circumstances, parties should exhaust the grievance procedure before filing ULP charges. Doing so keeps the issue within the collective bargaining framework and the purview of the parties, giving them the opportunity to resolve the conflict of their own accord. Once filed, a ULP charge transfers decision-making and resolution of the conflict to a third party.

ULPs have their place, and are a valid and useful component of the collective bargaining structure, but they cause significant stress to the labor-management relationship. They should be used only when a statutory obligation has not been met and where other options for resolution are absent or have been exhausted.

6.21   Effects of Grievances

Grievance management may not be the most pleasant thing representatives have to do, but grievances do serve a purpose in the labor-management relationship. They may also bring positive outcomes that may not otherwise be accessible to the parties.

- Grievances alert parties to problems in the workplace. Sometimes management first learns of an issue when a grievance is filed, and the union is first able to identify problematic workplace practices when forced to consider them in light of the contract. At other times, it is in the course of dealing with a grievance that parties may be able to recognize larger issues, such as patterns of conduct or outcomes that were immediately evident. Even where issues raised as grievances turn out to be mere gripes, they may provide enough information to allow the parties to identify an issue of concern which needs to be addressed.

- Engaging in the grievance procedure is a demonstration of good faith. The grievance procedure is an effective means by which both parties can keep each other accountable to their bargaining obligations, and focused on resolving issues as they arise.

- Grievances allow parties to test their contract language in a way that may not otherwise be possible, because they effectively highlight problems with the language. Conflicting provisions, ambiguous language, obsolete rules or gaps in contract language are some of the problems that may be brought to light through grievances. In some cases, resolution on the existing language may be possible, while in others the grievance will alert the parties that the language must be renegotiated. In either case, the grievance becomes the catalyst for the parties engaging in further collective bargaining to ensure their contract language meets their needs.

6.22 Grievance Procedures

The grievance procedure guides parties through the process from to beginning to end, providing multiple opportunities for resolution. Ideally, conflicts are resolved at the lowest possible level, with the least amount of disruption to the operations, and without needless delay or cost to the parties.

- <u>Decision Making</u>

    Many grievance procedures begin with an informal appeal, or seek to engage the first-level supervisor in resolving the issue. If resolution is not reached, the moving party has the ability to escalate the grievance so it will be addressed by individuals with greater authority in the organization.

The steps of the grievance procedure are not intended to be a form of rubber-stamping earlier decisions. The intent of the escalating steps is to allow the matter to reviewed anew by individuals with (ostensibly) greater objectivity and greater authority to effect resolution.

This escalation necessarily increases the separation between those actually responsible for and involved in the matter being grieved and those who will decide its outcome. This brings some benefits and some challenges to the process. The parties benefit from what ought to be a more objective perspective of the matter. However, this distance also has the potential to undermine resolution if the decision maker lacks understanding of the critical circumstances involved.

For instance, the department director, though empowered to adjust the grievance, may not be sufficiently acquainted with the operations of the work unit to determine whether some action taken by management was justified or what resolution might be most appropriate. Fortunately, representatives often are able to bridge such gaps by ensuring decision makers have the information needed to inform their decision-making.

- <u>Timelines</u>

    Timelines are set for the filing of the initial grievance, for scheduling and holding grievance meetings, for responding to the grievance at the various steps, and for advancing the grievance to the next available level of review. These timelines are critical to the effectiveness of the procedure as they facilitate the fundamental goals of timely and efficient resolution. Failure to meet the timelines undermines these goals and may prejudice one of the parties. For this reason, most contracts impose consequences in the event a party fails to meet a stated deadline.

    Many contracts provide for extension of grievance timelines by agreement. This is a valuable option when additional time is needed to properly address the grievance at that level, such as where additional information must be gathered or while the parties are discussing potential settlement. Where the activities causing the delay are conducive to resolving the issue, agreeing to hold timelines in abeyance is a show of good faith and fair dealing that serves both parties.

- <u>Procedural Deviations</u>
  Some grievance procedures will provide for skipping a step if there is insufficient authority to resolve issues at that step. While this may appear to contradict the tenet of resolution at the lowest possible level, it recognizes that resolution may not be possible at all if the resources and decision-making authority needed to resolve a particularly issue are not available.

  Disciplinary actions are one example of issues for which parties might agree to skipping steps in the grievance procedure. Depending on the organizational structure and level of discipline at issue, disciplinary grievances may need to be initiated at the higher steps of the grievance procedure, since it is unlikely a first-level supervisor will be able to overturn a decision made by a more senior manager. The grievance would then be filed at the level at which someone with the authority to review the manager's decision would be the decision-maker.

6.23 Grievance Pitfalls

While they may bring some benefits, grievances do cause stress in the workplace and on the relationship between parties. This reality makes it all the more important to understand their purpose and use them appropriately, in order to avoid exacerbating the impacts of conflicts.

When parties have an erroneous or unrealistic view of the grievance process and what it is intended, or able, to accomplish, the grievance process can be rendered unproductive. If supervisors see grievances as merely a nuisance or an affront to their authority, their response is likely to be unnecessarily defensive and may hinder resolution.

Similarly, misuse or abuse of the grievance procedure undermine its effectiveness. Tactics such as using the grievance procedure to punish or humiliate members of management, make unreasonable demands, or support employees' unjustifiable expectations or actions, is an abuse of the process. Such attempts are unproductive at best and can prove destructive to the workplace and the labor-management relationship.

Other missteps occur when parties use grievances as a substitute for proper advocacy. This may be the union representative who files unwarranted grievances because they do not want to tell their members when they are in the wrong, or the management representative who wants to avoid making a decision they know will be unpopular and instead tries to make the process to decide for them.

This type of advocacy-by-grievance occurs most often when the relationship between parties is so broken that collaboration and communication are no longer considered to be valid or desirable ways of interacting. Good faith bargaining is replaced by conflict conditioning, and the grievance procedure becomes the pointy weapon with which a party engages with their opponent. This is not a valid use of the grievance process, and is an expression of bad faith.

6.3 Alternative Dispute Resolution Methods

When parties have exhausted their own efforts at resolving conflicts, they must seek assistance outside of the labor-management relationship. The two main options available are mediation and arbitration.

6.31 Mediation

Mediation allows the parties to reach resolution with the assistance and guidance of a third party. Its greatest benefit is that the resolution is a product of the parties' own initiative and likely to be acceptable and adhered to by both labor and management. However, mediation efforts are not guaranteed to end in resolution, since the parties are under no obligation to reach agreement.

Parties should choose mediation if they believe a solution is within their reach, and they are able to offer reasonable alternatives that might be of value to the other party. When the dispute occurs during contract negotiation, mediation can help parties understand the opposing perspective and craft alternative solutions that may not be attainable through straight bargaining. Mediation may be used at any stage of a conflict, as long as the parties mutually agree to it, and may be attempted more than once for a single issue.

6.32 Arbitration

Arbitration does not rely on the parties' ability to resolve the issue, but turns decision-making over to a neutral third party. Arbitration has the benefit of bringing most matters to final conclusion because it does not require the concurrence of the disputants.

Arbitration is often the final step in the grievance procedure. Parties typically agree that the arbitrator's decision is final and binding, and not subject to appeal. Variations occur in some public sector environments, such as where arbitration results in advisory decisions which must then be approved by a governing body or court. Even in these situations, arbitration is generally viewed as being the end of the line for labor-management disputes.

The ability to bring matters to final resolution is especially valuable where a dispute has been protracted or has caused excessive upheaval or uncertainty in the workplace or the labor-management relationship. Bringing such disputes to an end is in the best interests of all involved, and this is something arbitration accomplishes quite well.

There are, however, times when even arbitration will not be able to resolve an issue for the parties. This is most often the case where the collective bargaining agreement does not contain the language that can meet the parties' needs. Such situations can only be cured through negotiation.
Arbitrators are limited by the existing terms of the parties' agreement and must enforce those terms faithfully. If the language one or both parties wish to implement does not already exist in the contract, the arbitrator will not have the power to enforce it through the grievance arbitration process, and may

not apply the existing language so as to have it serve a purpose the parties did not mutually intend.

Where the dispute arises in the context of negotiations, certain bargaining units may resort to interest arbitration in which the arbitrator formulates the terms of the collective bargaining agreement. Interest arbitration is only available in sectors in which strike action would be detrimental to the public interest, such as law enforcement and public transportation.

6.4 Dispute Resolution as Collective Bargaining

Dispute resolution in collective bargaining places the focus on honoring and maintaining the agreements made between the parties. The grievance procedure begins with the language and the terms to which the parties have agreed, and the dispute is ultimately resolved by applying the terms to which the parties have agreed. Regardless of the means parties use to reach resolve conflicts, their efforts, and the results of those efforts, ultimately affect the way they engage in collective bargaining moving forward.

Once a conflict has been resolved, the parties must incorporate the resolution, and any lessons learned along the way, into their practices to avoid a repeat of the conflict. In this way, conflict ultimately enriches and fortifies the labor-management relationship.

Even contentious labor-management relationships can be productive and effective at meeting collective bargaining goals. When labor and management approach issues in a manner that respects the rights of the other party and demonstrates good faith, much can be accomplished even in the midst of conflict.

NOTES — NEGOTIATIONS

NOTES — PRACTICE

NOTES — EMPLOYMENT

NOTES — OPERATIONS

NOTES — CONFLICT

INDEX

A

Accommodation...66, 105-106, 109

Arbitration............111 176-179

Attendance..........163

B

Balancing Test.......... 43-45

Bargaining History...... 25, 36, 41, 45, 73, 147

Bargaining Obligations...... 15-18, 20, 22, 23, 30, 42, 45, 46, 52, 57, 61, 62, 64, 65, 79, 166, 168, 169, 170

Bargaining Pitfalls..........45-51

Bargaining Units....26, 88, 95, 135, 140, 142, 160, 165

Bid Systems...........88

Breaks............28, 148, 150, 162

Building Credibility...... 76-77, 82

C

Call-Back..........156-157

Coaching............... 111-113, 117

Collaboration...62, 129, 159, 163, 176

Collective Bargaining... 12-16, 21, 23, 24, 27, 29, 30, 32, 46, 51, 60, 62, 64, 75, 80, 166, 169, 171, 180

Collective Bargaining Agreement....11, 21, 24, 36, 60, 65, 66, 67, 69, 70, 72, 73, 74, 91, 97, 111, 114, 141, 153, 158, 162, 167, 168, 178, 179

Community of Interests........25, 135

Commute Time......... 151-152

Compensable Time....147-149, 151

Compensation.......87, 114, 115, 134, 140, 142, 150, 151, 156, 158, 163

Concerted Activity...... 13-14, 16-19, 26

Confidential Employee... 138-139

Conflict Resolution...... 12, 70, 106, 165-167, 169, 171, 175, 176, 177, 179

D

Decision Bargaining...... 38, 39, 47, 49

Designated Representatives.....52, 139

Direct Dealing....55-56, 130

Disability..........104-106

Discipline..........110-119, 121-125, 137, 138

Dispute Resolution....70, 167, 166, 167, 176,179

Donning and Doffing.....149

Due Process....120-122

Duty of Fair Representation..50

E

Effects Bargaining....... 38, 40-42, 49

Emergency Response... 148, 156, 164

Employee Issues.103-109

End-Runs............53-55

External Law.........152

F

Failure to Bargain......42, 46-48

Family & Medical Leave......104, 107

Federal Service Labor-Management Relations Statute...............16

G

Good Faith Bargaining........ 19, 23, 46, 48, 51-60, 62, 170, 176

Grievance Pitfalls...... 175-176

Grievance Procedure... 70, 170-174, 179

Grievances..........12, 167-179

H

Hiring...................20, 85-88

I

Illegal Subjects of Bargaining......29-32, 51

Impact Bargaining...40, 42, 48

Information Request...... 57, 58

Initial Contract......33-34

Interest Arbitration......... 179

Interference..........18, 23

J

Job Classification...... 133-146

Job Posting...............87

Jurisdictional Issues...... 144-147

Just Cause............... 117-125

L

Labor Laws..........12, 14, 16, 24, 25,

Labor Management Committees......... 130-132

Last Chance Agreements......... 136-137

Leaves..................107, 157-158

Legal Troubles.......103, 109

Loudermill........121-123

M

Management Rights...... 20, 32, 161

Mandatory Subjects of Bargaining..........28-2 9, 31, 33, 38, 39, 41, 43, 47, 48, 152, 159, 164

Mediation.........176-177

Meet and Confer.......28, 33

Mental Health Issues........104, 108-109

Mid-Term Bargaining... 37-38, 46

Minimum Staffing.......86

Mis-classification......135

Mitigating and Aggravating Factors..........123-125

Mixed Practice..........73

N

National Labor Relations Act....15, 30

Negotiations.....27, 32, 39, 41, 45, 54, 56, 57, 58, 61, 81, 139, 153, 165, 179

Notice.......42, 47, 48, 49, 74, 111, 112, 118, 119, 121, 122, 153

O

Onboarding.........88-89

Ordinances..............69

Organizing..........18, 19, 23, 135, 136, 137

Orientation............ 88-90, 92

Overtime...28, 114, 154-157, 162, 163, 164

P

Past Practice.......70-75

Performance Assessment........95

Performance Management...92-102

Performance Reviews.....96-97

Permissive Subjects of Bargaining......329, 31, 40, 41, 43, 44, 47

Personal Protective Equipment (PPE)...... 159-160, 162

Policies...............11,29,38, 65, 67-70, 89, 93, 116, 158, 160, 161, 164

Premium Pay......155, 158

Probationary Periods..... 90-91, 101, 140

Progressive Discipline......112-116

Prohibited Subjects of Bargaining.........29, 30

R

Railway Labor Act......16

Ratifying Agreements.......59-60

Reassignment............ 101-102

Refusal to Bargain......48

Regulatory Environment....67, 142, 158

Remedial Plan......... 100-101

Reopeners...........37-38

Reserved Rights......31, 32, 85, 143, 161

Right to Representation... 120-121

Rights Bargaining.....38, 39, 47, 49

Rights of Employees...13, 18

S

Safety..........66, 93, 108, 115, 148, 156, 158-159

Safety-Sensitive Positions...150, 159

Schedules...........28, 39, 152, 153

Setting Expectations....92, 93, 95, 100, 118

Shift Extension......151, 155

Shifts Changes.........154

Sick Leave..............158

Standing.........122, 140

Strikes...............12, 21, 61, 179

Substance Abuse...... 104, 107, 108, 126

Successor Agreement... 36

Supervisors...........56, 76, 92, 93, 96, 97, 98, 99, 100, 111, 137, 138, 175

T

Timekeeping...........162

Training.........29, 88, 90, 91, 94, 95, 97, 98, 99, 100, 102, 146

U

Unfair Labor Practice... 22, 42, 47, 48, 50, 55, 62, 168

Unit Clarification...... 137, 139

Unpaid Time........114, 149-150, 157

V

Vacation............114, 158

W

Wages 25, 28, 43, 44, 95, 96, 155, 159, 162

Waiver of Right to Bargain............49-50

Weingarten Rights......... 121

Workplace Expectations............97, 115-116, 125, 162

Work Rules.......172-176

Working Conditions...... 25, 28, 31, 44, 69, 96, 143, 147

Working Hours.........43, 147, 148, 149, 150, 152, 153, 156, 157

Z

Zero-Tolerance......... 116-117

Zipper Clause.........34, 37, 74

Made in the USA
Middletown, DE
26 August 2024

59753405R00116